Heart of Darkness

publisher
Mike Richardson

series editors
Rachel Penn
& Mike Hansen

collection editor
Chris Warner

collection designer
Amy Arendts

English-language version produced by Studio Proteus for Dark Horse Comics, Inc.

This book collects issues thirty-five through forty-two of the Dark Horse comic-book series, *Blade of the Immortal*.

Published by Dark Horse Manga
A division of Dark Horse Comics, Inc.
10956 SE Main Street
Milwaukie, OR 97222

www.darkhorse.com

To find a comics shop in your area, call the Comic Shop Locator Service toll-free at 1-888-266-4226

First edition: April 2001
ISBN: 1-56971-531-9

5 7 9 10 8 6 4

Printed in Canada

BLADE OF THE IMMORTAL

art and story
HIROAKI SAMURA

translation
Dana Lewis & Toren Smith

lettering and retouch
Tomoko Saito

Heart of Darkness

DARK HORSE MANGA™

ABOUT THE TRANSLATION

The Swastika

The main character in *Blade of the Immortal*, Manji, has taken the "crux gammata" as both his name and his personal symbol. This symbol is also known as the *swastika*, a name derived from the Sanskrit *svastika* (meaning "welfare," from *su* — "well" + *asti* "he is"). As a symbol of prosperity and good fortune, the swastika was widely used throughout the ancient world (for example, appearing often on Mesopotamian coinage), including North and South America and has been used in Japan as a symbol of Buddhism since ancient times. To be precise, the symbol generally used by Japanese Buddhists is the *sauvastika*, which moves in a counterclockwise direction and is called the *manji* in Japanese. The arms of the *swastika*, which point in a clockwise direction, are generally considered a solar symbol. It was this version (the *hakenkreuz*) that was perverted by the Nazis. The *sauvastika* generally stands for night, and often for magical practices. It is important that readers understand that the swastika has ancient and honorable origins, and it is those that apply to this story, which takes place in the 18th century [ca. 1782–3]. *There is no anti-Semitic or pro-Nazi meaning behind the use of the symbol in this story. Those meanings did not exist until after 1910.*

The Artwork

The creator of *Blade of the Immortal* requested that we make an effort to avoid mirror-imaging his artwork. Normally, Westernized manga are first copied in a mirror-image in order to facilitate the left-to-right reading of the pages. However, Mr. Samura decided that he would rather see his pages reversed via the technique of cutting up the panels and re-pasting them in reverse order. While we feel that this often leads to problems in panel-to-panel continuity, we place primary importance on the wishes of the creator. Therefore, most of *Blade of the Immortal* has been produced using the "cut and paste" technique. There are, of course, some sequences where it was impossible to do this, and mirror-imaged panels or pages were used.

The Sound Effects & Dialogue

Since some of Mr. Samura's sound effects are integral parts of the illustrations, we decided to leave those in their original Japanese. We hope readers will view the unretouched sound effects as essential portions of Mr. Samura's extraordinary artwork. In addition, Mr. Samura's treatment of dialogue is quite different from that featured in typical samurai manga and is considered to be one of the features that has made *Blade* such a hit in Japan. Mr. Samura has mixed a variety of linguistic styles in this fantasy story, with some characters speaking in the mannered style of old Japan while others speak as if they were street-corner punks from a bad area of modern-day Tokyo. The anachronistic slang used by some of the characters in the English translation reflects the unusual mix of speech patterns from the original Japanese text.

HEART OF DARKNESS
Part 1

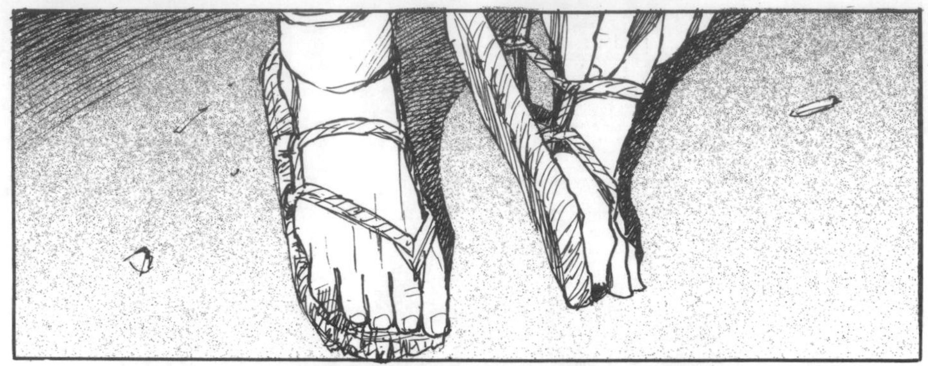

whew...
I'M BEAT.

YO! ANYBODY HOME?!
ABAYAMA SŌSUKE IS HERE, UNDERSTAND?! YOUR NEW BOSS!

AH! WE'VE BEEN AWAITING YOU, SIR!

WHO THE HELL ARE YOU?
I'VE JUST JOINED, SIR.

WHAT'S YOUR NAME, SON?
MAKOTO, SIR.
AND YOUR FAMILY NAME?

ACTUALLY. SIR...I DON'T HAVE ONE. WE WERE PEASANTS...
A PEASANT, HUH? I'LL BE DAMNED.

...THEY'RE BOTH THE SAME TO THE GOOD OLD *ITTŌ-RYŪ*, EH?
THAT MAKES YOU NUMBER TWO. DAMN... AN EDICT FROM THE SHŌGUN, A HORSE TURD ON THE ROAD...

I SUPPOSE I COULD, SIR.
BUT FOR NOW, JUST "MAKOTO" IS ENOUGH.
WHY NOT JUST PICK SOME NAME, LIKE MAGATSU DID?
SO...

--*TELL ME HOW FUSANO AND MOROZUMI DIED.*
SO TELL ME, SON, FROM BEGINNING TO END--

......
......

IF I TAKE THAT ONE, THEN I TAKE THAT THERE, AND THERE, AND... NO. NO, WAIT. I TAKE THAT ONE, AN'...

HYAKURIN, MA'AM... IF I MIGHT SUGGEST--
SHADDUP!

......
UM...
IF YOU DO THAT, MA'AM...
...IT'S THE SAME OLD THING.
SEE...?
GNIPH!

NO, NO, I SWEAR! I MEAN, A SIMPLE GAME LIKE THIS... NOT EVEN FOR MONEY OR NOTHIN'? WH-WHY SHOULD I *CHEAT*, MA'AM?
DON'T YOU SCREW WITH ME, YOU CHEATING LITTLE JERK!

THEN WHY CAN'T I WIN EVEN *ONCE*, GODDAMIT?!
G-GOOD QUESTION, MA'AM...

AH... THE DOOR?
YES, SIR?
YOU BETTER NOT TRY AND PULL ANY OF THAT "WIN AND RUN" CRAP, BUDDY!

YO, SHINRIJI.

?!
YOU GUYS LIVE IN A PUBLIC BATH?
YEAH. BUT IT'S CLOSED FOR NOW.

AH, HELLO, SIR. DID--

kchak

ER... WELCOME...

AT LEAST TAKE DOWN THE DAMN *SIGN*, YOU IDIOT.
AH? Oh, RIGHT... SORRY, SIR!

VERY PLEASED TO MEET YOU, SIR.
EH?! Uh...NO, THE P-PLEASURE'S MINE, MISS!

GEE... IT'S SORTA...
...SORTA GRIM IN HERE.

IF I THINK ABOUT IT...
YAAWN
...ALL THESE GUYS WANT IS MANJI AND HIS ABILITIES.
THAT'S WHY THEY INVITED HIM RIGHT INTO THEIR HIDEOUT.

AND TO THEM, I'M KINDA LIKE, "WHAT THE HECK IS SHE DOING HERE...?"

AS FAR AS I'M CONCERN-ED...
...THE MORE ALLIES WE HAVE, THE BETTER. BUT EVEN SO... THESE GUYS...

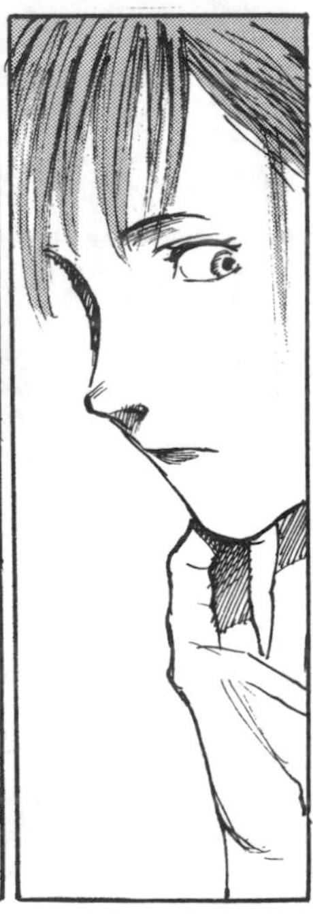

UM...
......

HUH! LOOK AT 'EM.

FOUR GUYS SITTIN' AROUND, ALL STONE-FACED AND TOUGH-LIKE.
IT'D MAKE ANYONE UNCOMFORT-ABLE, KID!

koff

SO... SHALL WE SEAL THE DEAL WITH A DRINK?

IT'S GOOD STUFF, TOO-- STRAIGHT FROM ITAMI.

AND SOME PLUM WINE FOR YOU. THAT OKAY?
OH! YES, THANK YOU!

HERE YOU ARE, MISTER "HUNDRED-MAN KILLER."
LOOK...

...WE AIN'T EVEN DECIDED IF WE'RE WORKING TOGETHER, YET.
SO DON'T YOU GO EXPECTING THIS TO BE "SEALING" ***NOTHING.***

HUH! TIGHT-ASSED BASTARD, AREN'T YOU? STILL, NO MATTER.
THIS STUFF SHOULD LOOSEN YOU UP.

NO CHARGE FOR THE PERSONALIZED POISON TASTING, HON.
.....
.....

HERE.
AH, GREAT.

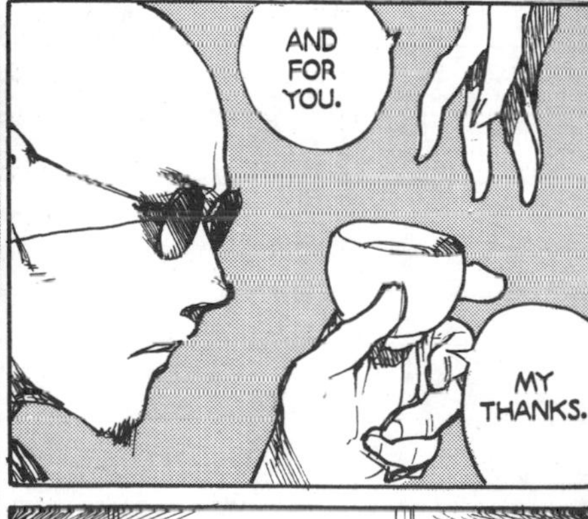
AND FOR YOU.
MY THANKS.

HERE... YOU, TOO.
DON'T GET ANY BIG IDEAS.
HUH?!
BUT... BUT... BUT...

NOW THEN...

C'MON--
GIVE IT BACK.
HOW LONG DOES IT TAKE YOU TO READ A FEW PAGES, ANYWAYS?!
HUH?!
......
......
HERE.

THIS IS WHAT WE CAN OFFER YOU IN EXCHANGE FOR THAT SWORD ARM OF YOURS.

GO AHEAD-- LOOK IT OVER FIRST.
WE'LL GET YOUR ANSWER WHEN YOU'RE DONE.

......
......
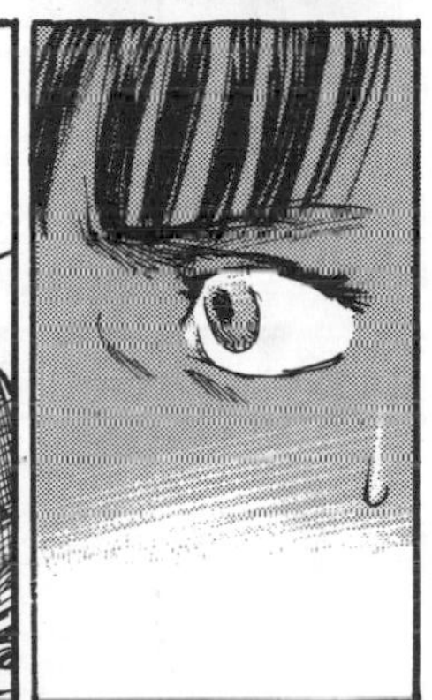

......
......

OKAY, YOU GUYS.
I GOT TWO THINGS I WANT TO ASK.

JUST WHAT THE HELL *ARE* YOU?
THAT'S *ONE.*

THAT DEPENDS ON WHAT "*WHAT*" MEANS, HEY?
WE'RE THE *MUGAI-RYŪ.*

BUT AS SWORD SCHOOLS GO, WELL...
...AS YOU CAN SEE, WE DON'T HAVE A *DŌJŌ*, OR INSTRUCTORS, OR STUDENTS.
HMM... I GUESS, COME RIGHT DOWN TO IT, WE'RE BUMS.
NO SHIT. OKAY, THEN-- NUMBER TWO.

THIS STUFF YOU GOT HERE ABOUT ANOTSU GETTING THREE DIFFERENT TRAVEL PASSES IN HIS OWN NAME...
...HIS ROUTE...

...THAT HE'LL HAVE AT LEAST FOUR *KENSHI* WITH HIM...

...AND THE REASON HE'S GOING TO KAGA...
...IS THAT HE'S GOING TO MERGE THE *ITTŌ-RYŪ* WITH ANOTHER *DŌJŌ*.

C'MON! WHAT IS THIS CRAP?
JUST SOME RUMORS...
...YOU BUMS HEARD BLOWING ON THE WIND?

OUR RELATIVE POSITIONS SEEM TO BE SIMILAR...
...MISTER MANJI.

BUT WHEN YOU GET DOWN TO DETAILS...
...WELL, THAT'S WHERE THE DEVIL IS.

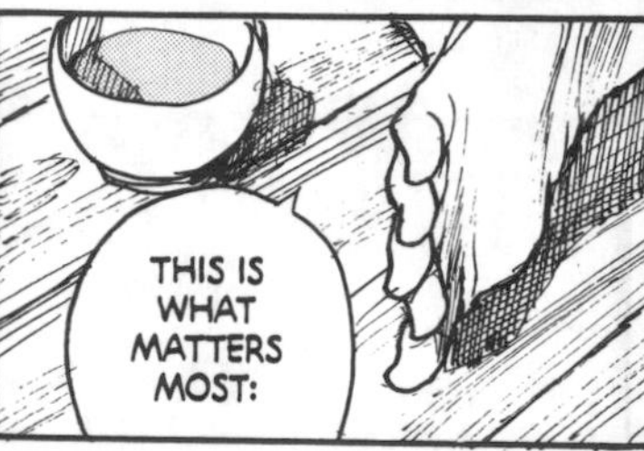
THIS IS WHAT MATTERS MOST:

THERE ARE JUST TWO OF YOU...
...AND *SIX* OF US.

FOUR OF US RIGHT HERE, IN THIS ROOM.
AND AS FOR THE REMAINING TWO, ONE IS PART TIME, AND THE LAST ONE...

WHERE DO YOU THINK HE IS, YOUNG MISS?
HUH?! WELL, Um... Er...

I... I'M JUST GUESSING, BUT...
...I MEAN, IT'S A CRAZY IDEA, BUT--

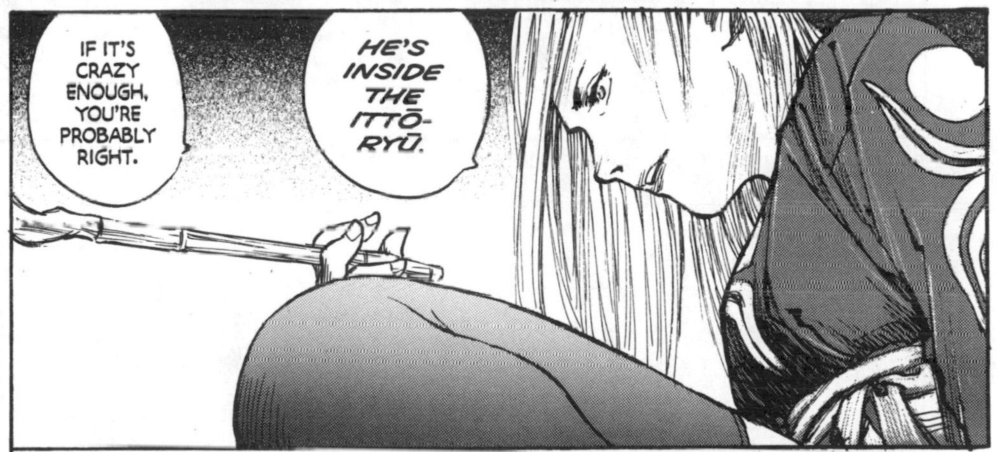
HE'S INSIDE THE ITTŌ-RYŪ.
IF IT'S CRAZY ENOUGH, YOU'RE PROBABLY RIGHT.

WHAT WE HAVE WRITTEN HERE IS INFORMATION DIRECT FROM OUR MAN.
WE FIGURE A GOOD EIGHTY PERCENT OF IT IS RELIABLE.

EIGHTY PERCENT?!
AN INSIDE JOB SHOULD BE *ONE HUNDRED PERCENT*.

MANJI.
I THOUGHT I TOLD YOU *YESTER-DAY*, MAN!
THAT STUFF ABOUT US WHACKING A FEW *ITTŌ-RYŪ* DUDES, HEY?
BY NOW ANOTSU MUST'A HEARD ABOUT IT.
IF HE'S SMART ENOUGH TO WORRY ABOUT AN INFORMER...
...HE MAY EVEN TRY TO SNOW HIS OWN MEN.
SO IF YA THINK ABOUT IT... FIGURE EIGHTY PERCENT, HEY?

IN OTHER WORDS, IT'S EIGHTY PERCENT BECAUSE YOU GUYS DIDN'T THINK BEFORE YOU STRUCK.
SHEE-IT... DAMN AMATEURS.
NYA HA HAHA! WELL, I FIGURE...
...NO USE CRYING OVER SPILT MILK, HUH?

OKAY, THIS THIRD PAGE HERE-- "ASKED TWO OR THREE TIMES TO GO PURCHASE WOMEN'S KIMONO, SASH, AND STRAW SUN HAT."
WHAT'S THAT ALL ABOUT?

OH, YEAH, THAT STUFF.

WE'VE HAD HIM WRITE DOWN EVERYTHING THAT'S HAPPENED AT THE *ITTŌ-RYŪ*'S **HQ**, THE TEMPO *DŌJŌ*, FOR THE PAST COUPLE OF WEEKS...
...NO MATTER HOW SMALL.

IT MAY NOT HAVE ANYTHING TO DO WITH ANYTHING.
BUT TUCK IT AWAY IN YOUR BRAIN, ANY-HOW.

MAYBE THEY'RE PRESENTS OR SOMETHING FOR HIS TRIP...
WOMEN'S CLOTHES? I THOUGHT THEY DON'T EVEN HAVE A MAID...
AND SO...
HOW ABOUT IT, MANJI?
A SWAP... OUR INFO FOR YOUR SWORD.
C'MON-- IT'S A SWEET LITTLE DEAL.
YOU KNOW THE ONLY REASONABLE ANSWER.
SO YOU MIGHT AS WELL GIVE IT TO US.

IS THAT ALL?
?
YOU GUYS...

WHEN YOU ASK SOMEONE TO HELP YOU OUT, FIRST THINGS *FIRST*.
YOU GOTTA PUT *ALL* YOUR CARDS ON THE TABLE. AIN'T THAT SO?

AND THEN...
...THERE'S THIS BUILDING, HERE.

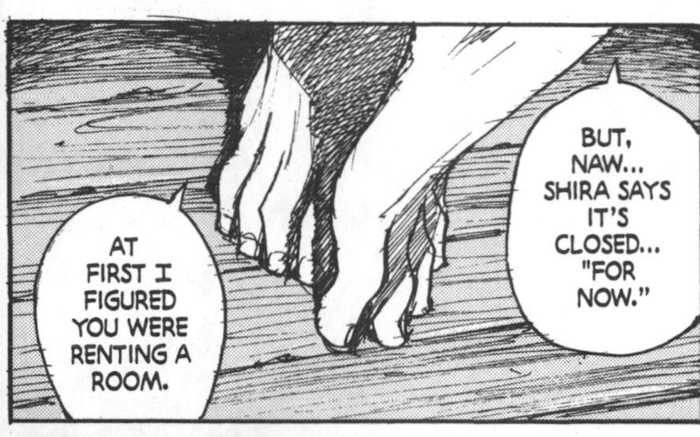
BUT, NAW... SHIRA SAYS IT'S CLOSED... "FOR NOW."
AT FIRST I FIGURED YOU WERE RENTING A ROOM.

AND I CAN SEE IT'S NOT SOME ROTTING OLD DUMP.
WHICH MEANS YOU GUYS PROBABLY OWN IT.

YEAH, IT MUST HAVE BEEN TOUGH, ALL RIGHT.
TOUGH FOR A BUNCH OF RŌNIN WITHOUT ANY STUDENTS AND NO WORK I CAN SEE TO BUY A NICE LITTLE HIDEOUT LIKE THIS, EH?

UNLESS, THAT IS... THEY GOT SOMEONE *REAL BIG* BEHIND THEM.

fap
......
......
NN!

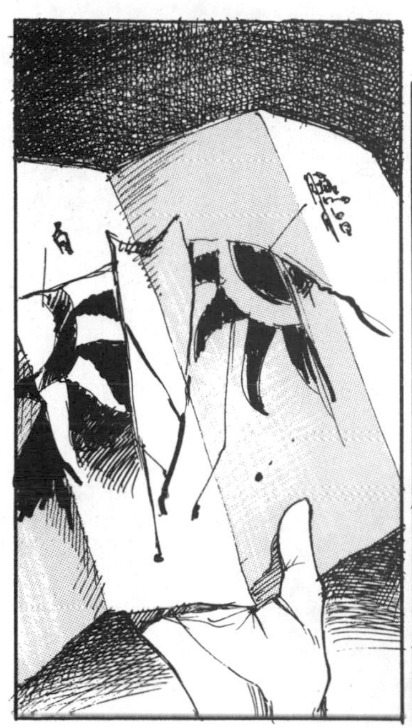

WHAT'S THIS...?

THE BASTARD WHO MURDERED O-REN? THAT'S THE KIMONO HE WAS WEARING.
THREE DAYS AGO, ANY-WAY.

YOU CAN KEEP IT. WHAT YOU DO WITH IT...
...IS YOUR BUSI-NESS.

WHY...? WHY'D YOU LEAVE HER OUT HERE...
...ON THE DIRT?

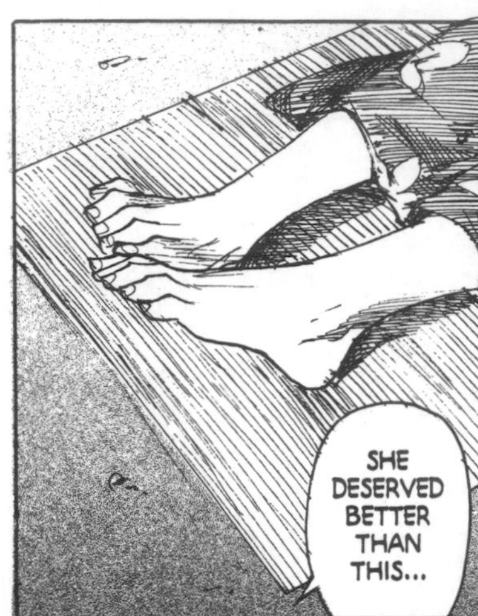
SHE DESERVED BETTER THAN THIS...

HEY, WE JUST CHOSE THE COLDEST PLACE, THAT'S ALL!
JUST IN CASE SOME DAMN JERK MAYBE FELT LIKE COMING BACK!

BECAUSE WE DIDN'T WANT YOU TO SEE...
...H-HER POOR BODY STARTING TO *ROT!*

DAMN IT!! IF YOU WEREN'T ALWAYS RUNNING OFF DOING YOUR OWN STUPID CRAP...
...THIS WOULD *NEVER* HAVE HAPPENED!

POOR O-REN... *DAMN* IT!
SHE JUST WANTED TO BE WITH YOU, ALWAYS. JUST THAT. NOTHING MORE.

YOU WITH YOUR BIG SWORD AND BIG TALK-- WHAT DID YOU EVER DO FOR HER?!
WAS THAT SUCH A BIG, BIG DREAM?! WAS IT SO MUCH TO ASK?! WHAT FUCKING GOOD ARE YOU *KENSHI*, ANYWAY?!

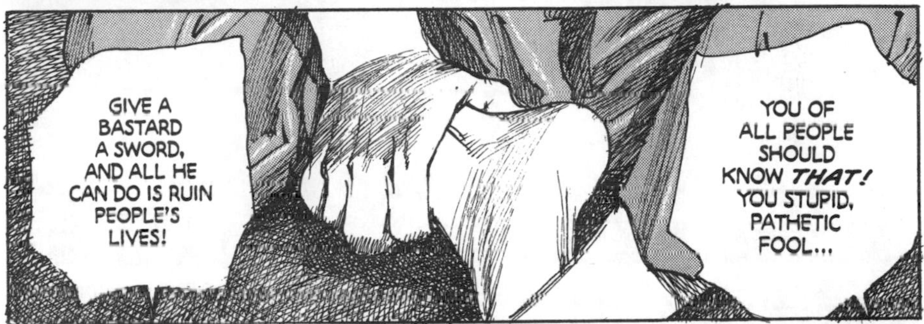
YOU OF ALL PEOPLE SHOULD KNOW *THAT!* YOU STUPID, PATHETIC FOOL...
GIVE A BASTARD A SWORD, AND ALL HE CAN DO IS RUIN PEOPLE'S LIVES!

BLAM
JUST *GET OUT!*

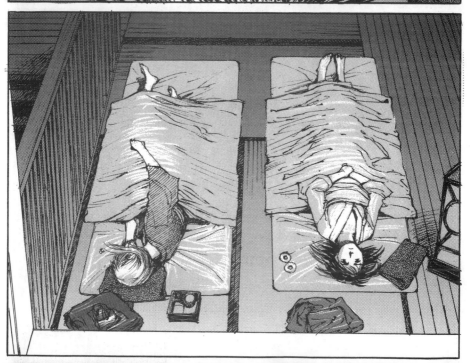

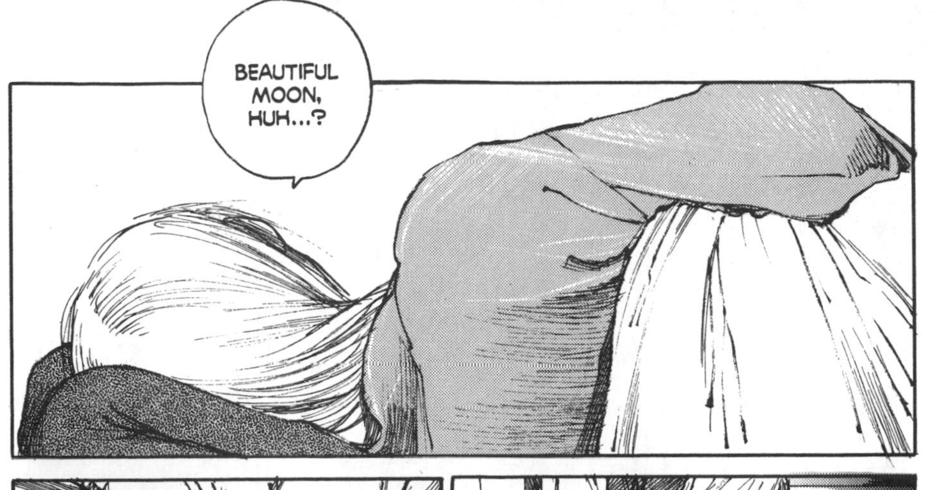
BEAUTIFUL MOON, HUH...?

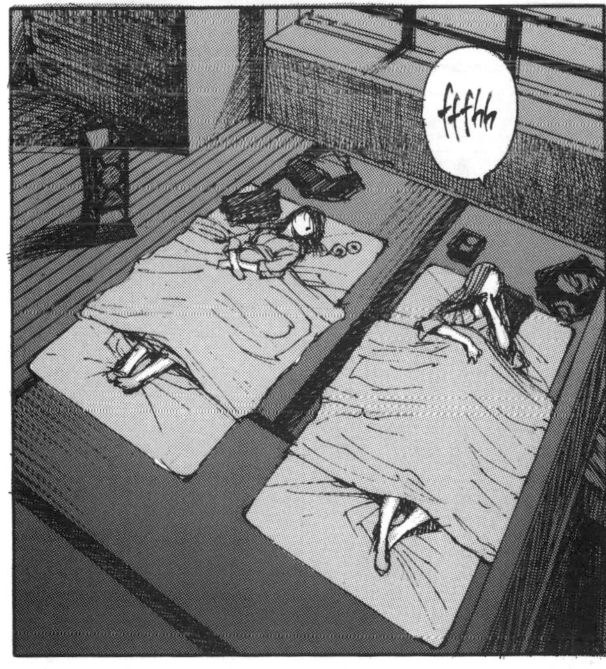
ffffhh

SO, LITTLE GIRL...
WANT A PUFF?

MMM... IT MAKES YOU FEEL SO CALM.
PUTS YOU RIGHT TO SLEEP.

MY HANDS AND FEET, GETTING COLDER AND COLDER...

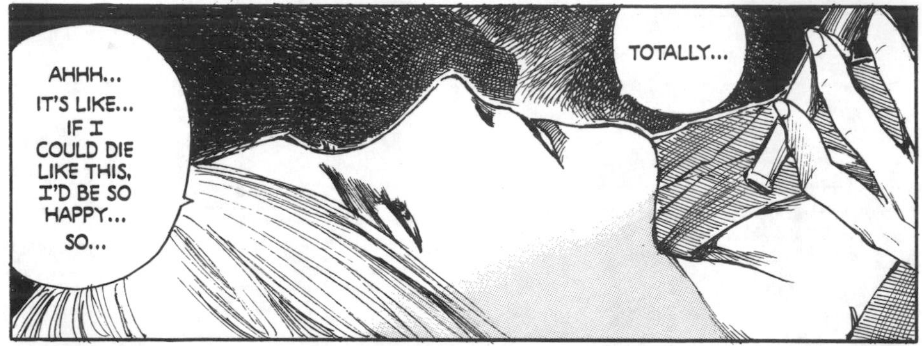
TOTALLY...
AHHH... IT'S LIKE... IF I COULD DIE LIKE THIS, I'D BE SO HAPPY... SO...

HA... ......

....!

JUST LIKE THAT!
HA, HA! I SEE.
UM... THEN...
MAYBE JUST A PUFF?
NOT YOUR MOUTH-- BREATHE IT INTO YOUR LUNGS.
AND THEN COUNT TO FIVE.
OOH, IT'S BITTER!
AH... OKAY.
ffffff
ffffh
ONE...♥
WHOOPS! NO, NO, NO...!

HUHECCH!!
HAGCCH!
KOFF
KOFF
koff
koff
YOU'RE SUPPOSED TO HOLD IT, HON!

HEH, HEH...

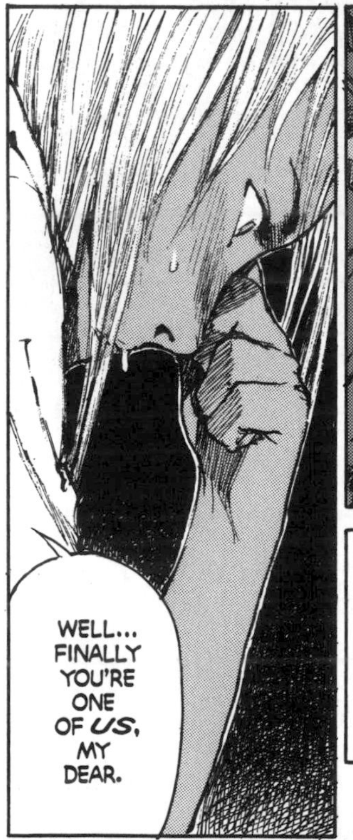
WELL... FINALLY YOU'RE ONE OF *US*, MY DEAR.

HUH...?!

SORRY, SWEETIE... BUT...
THIS IS HOW WE INITIATE NEW PEOPLE.

...THIS WAY WE MAKE SURE WE'VE ALL GOT SOMETHING ON EACH OTHER.
IN OTHER WORDS... IF WORST COMES TO WORST...

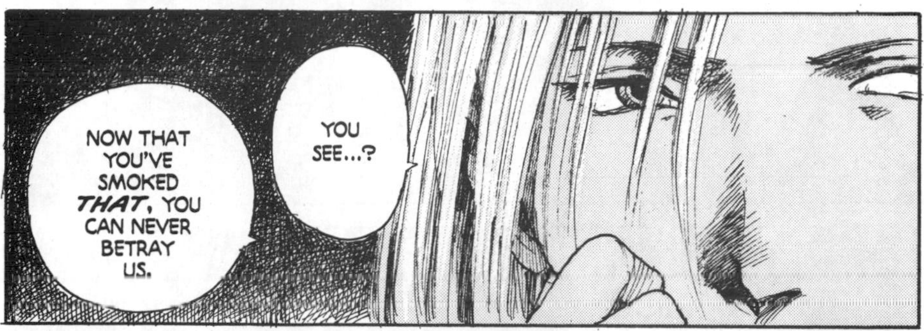
YOU SEE...?
NOW THAT YOU'VE SMOKED *THAT*, YOU CAN NEVER BETRAY US.

!!

YOU MEAN... THIS...

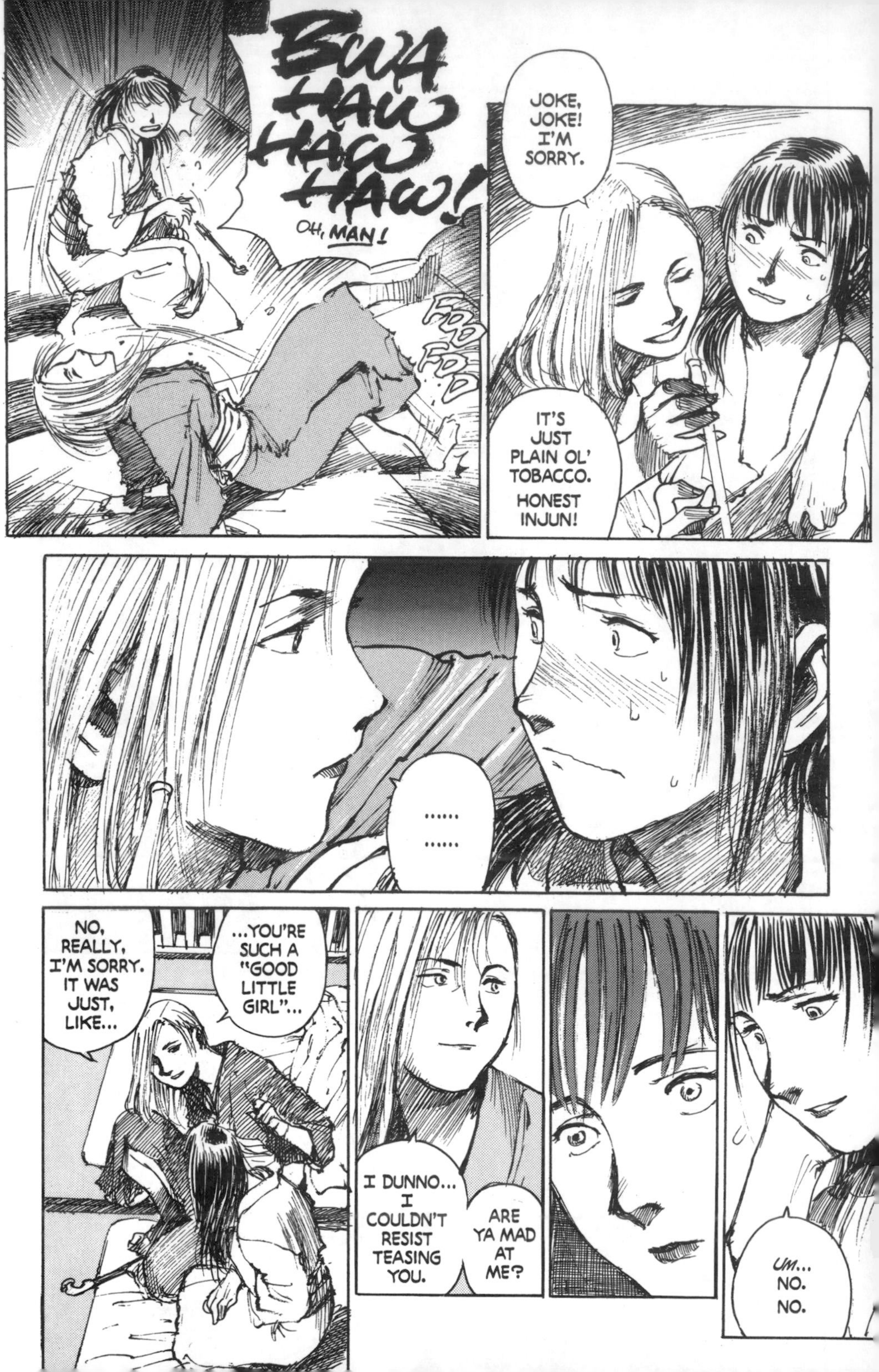

BWA HAW HAW HAW!
OH, MAN!
JOKE, JOKE! I'M SORRY.
IT'S JUST PLAIN OL' TOBACCO.
HONEST INJUN!

......
......

NO, REALLY, I'M SORRY. IT WAS JUST, LIKE...
...YOU'RE SUCH A "GOOD LITTLE GIRL"...
I DUNNO... I COULDN'T RESIST TEASING YOU.
ARE YA MAD AT ME?
UM... NO. NO.

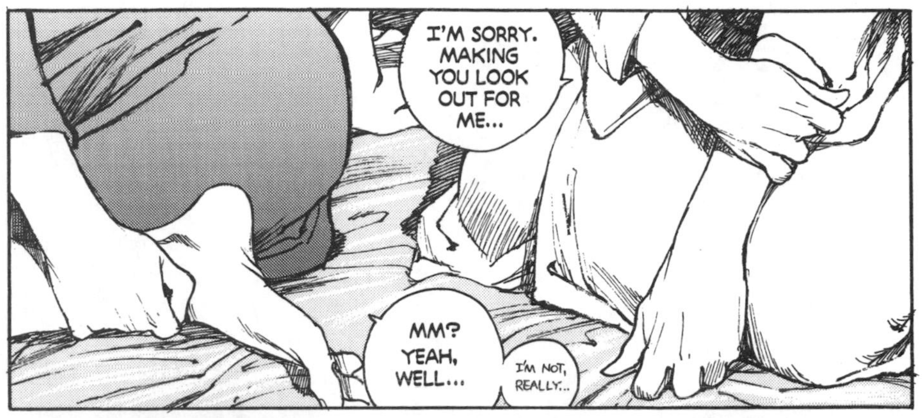
I'M SORRY. MAKING YOU LOOK OUT FOR ME...
MM? YEAH, WELL...
I'M NOT, REALLY...

...THINGS TAKE ON A LIFE OF THEIR OWN.
AND I... I JUST DON'T KNOW WHAT TO DO.

IT'S JUST...
LIKE, BEFORE I CAN EVEN GET MY HEAD AROUND IT...

YEAH, MUST BE PRETTY SCARY, JOINING UP WITH A BUNCH OF UNKNOWNS LIKE US.
THAT'S NOT WHAT I MEANT.
HUH? OH, NO...

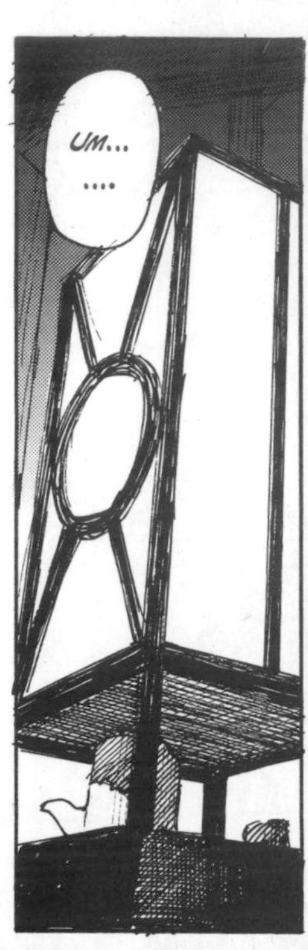
UM...
....

YEAH...?
THIS AFTER-NOON... WHAT MANJI SAID...?

OH, RIGHT.

YOU KNOW, I THOUGHT HE WAS DUMBER THAN THAT.
I SURE DID.

THEN...
SORRY!
I CAN'T TELL YOU RIGHT NOW.

MAYBE ONCE THIS JOB IS DONE...
...AND WE'VE KNOCKED DOWN THE WALLS BETWEEN US...

THEN I CAN TELL YOU WHO WE REALLY ARE...
AND...
...THE REAL REASON WE'RE AFTER THE *ITTŌ-RYŪ*.

SOMETIMES I FIND MYSELF THINKING, LIKE...
...THERE ARE THINGS IN THE WORLD YOU DON'T ***NEED*** TO KNOW, AND SOME THINGS IT'S BETTER ***NOT*** TO KNOW.

UM, HYAKU-RIN... ARE YOU, LIKE...
...ARE YOU EVERY-ONE'S BOSS...?
HUH? WHY?

IT'S JUST, I DUNNO... THE WAY YOU SAID THINGS.
AND YOU'RE REALLY YOUNG, BUT YOU'VE GOT SO MUCH PRE-SENCE...

HA, HA... THANKS. BUT I'VE BEEN AROUND A WHILE, DEAR.
TRY ***TEN YEARS*** LONGER THAN YOU.

YEAH, I USED TO HAVE A FAMILY.
ACK! NO WAY! AND SHE STILL DRESSES LIKE THAT?!
I EVEN HAD CHILDREN, YOU KNOW... TWO OF THEM.

WOW!
GEE. SO, WHAT ARE YOUR CHILDREN DOING NOW?

HYAKU-RIN...?

TELL ME, RIN.
WHAT'S UP WITH YOU AND THAT GUY?

HUH?!
I MEAN, HOW IS HE IN THE SACK?

WHA--?! B-BUT... WE...
HE'S TEN YEARS OLDER THAN ME!!
OH, YEAH. RIGHT.
AND WHAT'S YER POINT...?

MANJI IS JUST MY BODY-GUARD.
HE'S HELPING ME GET REVENGE.

REVENGE? FOR WHAT?
MY PARENTS. THE ITTŌ-RYŪ...

.....
.....
Ah, I SEE. IT'S PRETTY AWFUL, ISN'T IT? LOSING YOUR FAMILY...

GOOD!
WELL, IF HE'S JUST YOUR BODYGUARD, THEN IT'S NO BIG DEAL.

'CAUSE YOU'LL SUFFER FOR ***YEARS***, RIN...

...IF YOU EVER FALL FOR A GUY LIKE THAT.

OH...?

...? B- BUT...

HE... HE'S NOT...
...A ***BAD*** MAN.

YEAH, HE ***LOOKS***, YOU KNOW...
...HE ***LOOKS*** LIKE THAT.

AND THAT "HUNDRED MAN KILLER" STUFF IS TRUE, I GUESS.
BUT I'VE NEVER ONCE SEEN HIM KILL ANYONE WHO WASN'T "ARMED AND DANGER-OUS."

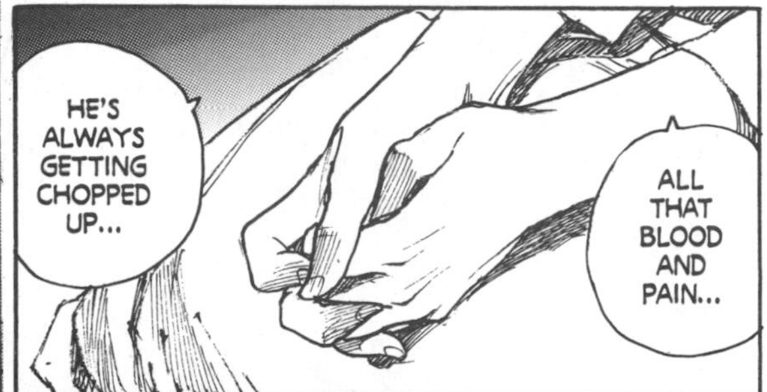
HE'S ALWAYS GETTING CHOPPED UP...
ALL THAT BLOOD AND PAIN...

JUST BECAUSE I'M SO WEAK.
HE'S ALWAYS... HE'S ALWAYS LIKE THAT...

LISTEN UP, KID.

IF YOU'RE ALWAYS BEING PROTECTED THAT WAY BY SOME TOUGH GUY...

...YOU'RE NEVER GOING TO BE STRONG ***YOURSELF***. RIGHT?

YEAH, WELL, WHAT-EVER.

C'MON-- TIME TO HIT THE SACK.

NO!
NO!!

NOOOOOO!

IT'S JUST... HER LITTLE PROBLEM.

......
......

FORGET IT.
!

HYAKU-RIN!
hahh
AH!

AAH!
UHHN

SHRIKK

hahh
hahh

huhh
hahh

......
......
......
hff

I... I'M SORRY.
D-DON'T WORRY. THIS JUST HAPPENS... SOME-TIMES...

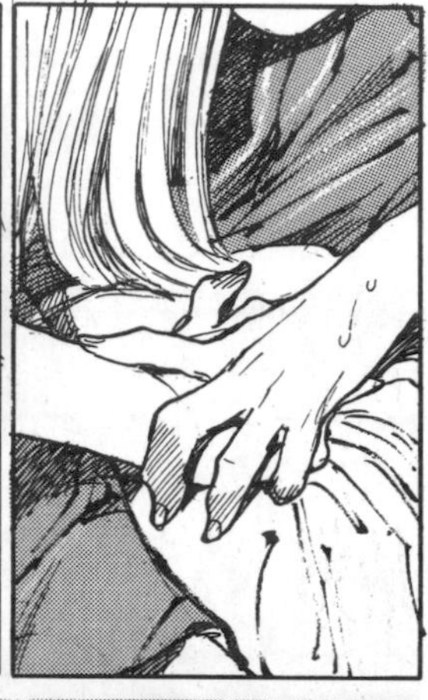

WAS IT... A BAD DREAM?

RIN, HONEY...
JUST NEVER... *NEVER* FALL FOR A SAMURAI...
?

HELLO? IT'S ABOUT THAT TIME.
ARE YOU ALMOST READY?

.....

SHKK
EXCUSE ME...

AH?!
OOPS! I... I'M SORRY!

S-SORRY ABOUT THAT!

?

WELL, WELL!

HEART OF DARKNESS
Part 2

MASTER ABAYAMA...? I BROUGHT YOU SOME TEA.

SIR...?
AH... OKAY.

ER... DON'T YOU LIKE TEA, SIR?
I DIDN'T SAY THAT, BOY.
IT'S JUST THAT... NIBBLING AT THESE *YŌKAN* SWEETS OR THE LIKE...

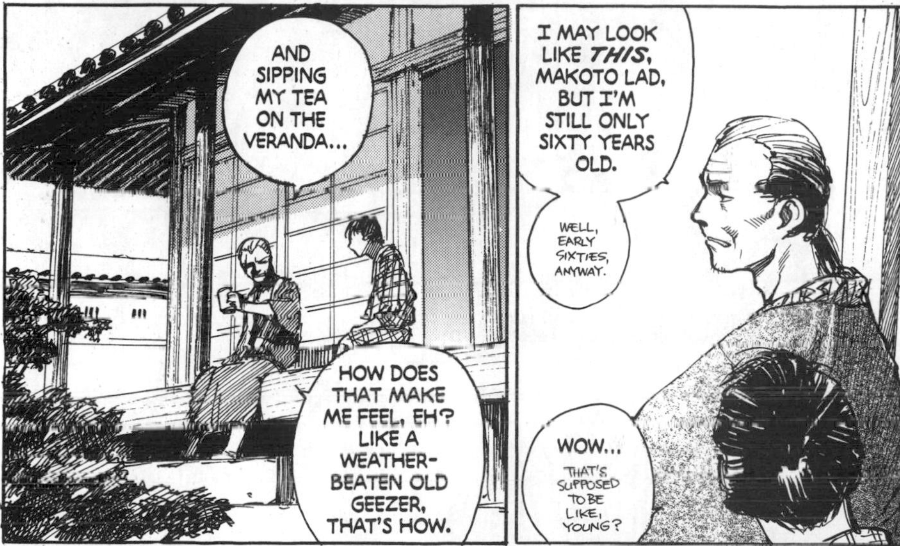
AND SIPPING MY TEA ON THE VERANDA...
HOW DOES THAT MAKE ME FEEL, EH? LIKE A WEATHER-BEATEN OLD GEEZER, THAT'S HOW.
I MAY LOOK LIKE *THIS*, MAKOTO LAD, BUT I'M STILL ONLY SIXTY YEARS OLD.
WELL, EARLY SIXTIES, ANYWAY.
WOW... THAT'S SUPPOSED TO BE LIKE, YOUNG?

NOW THAT YOU MENTION IT, DID THE BOSS...?
YEAH. THIS MORNING.

STILL, THOUGH... WHEN I SEE THAT LITTLE WIMP OF A KID MY OLD FRIEND ANOTSU SABURŌ LEFT IN MY CARE...
...AND THERE HE IS, RUNNING THE WHOLE *ITTŌ-RYŪ*... I THINK TO MYSELF--MAYBE THE TIME'S COME FOR ME TO RETIRE AT LAST.

SO, UM... WERE THEY REALLY FOR HIM TO DRESS UP IN?
THOSE KIMONO I BOUGHT, I MEAN?

YEAH.
HIS OWN IDEA.

BY THE WAY, SON...
I DIDN'T SEE YOU AROUND THIS MORNING.

HUH? OH, THAT.
I WENT DOWN TO UMEYA'S TO ORDER MORE OIL.

IT WAS DAMN CRAZY AROUND HERE, GETTING EVERYONE READY TO GO.
THAT WASN'T THE GREATEST TIMING, YOU KNOW.
YES, SIR. SORRY, SIR.

whewww...

THIS SMELL...

HE EVEN USED *MAKE-UP...?*

......?
STRANGE.
WHY ARE THERE STILL WOMEN'S CLOTHES...?

SO THIS IS NAITO SHINJUKU, *HMM?*

SOMETIMES IT FEELS LIKE WE'VE WALKED ALL OVER ***EVERY-WHERE.***

BUT I GUESS, EVEN NOW...
...WE'VE NEVER LEFT EDO, NOT EVEN ONCE.
HAVE WE...?

SHEESH... LOOK AT HIM. HOW CAN ***ANYONE***...
...SLEEP SO MUCH?

...!?

EEK!

......
......

WHAT THE *HELL* WERE YOU DOING?!

Uh... ER...
IT'S LIKE...
JUST CLEANING YOUR EARS, Y'KNOW? LIKE THIS?
FEELS GOOD!
YOU WOKE ME UP FOR *THAT*?

I'M SORRY! BUT, *UM*... SINCE YOU'RE UP, GOT A SEC?
JUST A SEC!

I MEAN, IT'S STILL LIGHT OUT, AND... AND...
CAN WE...*UM*... TALK A BIT?

BEING HERE ALL ALONE... GETS TO ME.
HA, HA...

......
......

HA, HA HA...?
EARWIGS, MAYBE?
NO PROBLEM-- MAKES IT WORTH THE DIG!

OKAY, GO AHEAD. BUT DON'T GET GROSSED OUT BY WHAT YOU FIND.

RIN.
WHAT ARE YOU SO JITTERY ABOUT.
ME?

OF MEETING ANOTSU.
YOU'RE *AFRAID*, RIGHT?

VERY.
Y... YES.

IT'S NOT THAT I'M REALLY AFRAID OF HIM, BUT...

MANJI? I THINK I'VE FIGURED OUT HOW TO CONQUER THEM.
MY *WEAKNESSES*, I MEAN.

WELL, THE STUFF IN MY HEAD, ANYWAY.
Hmm
STILL NOT QUITE THERE, YET.
MY SWORD WORK... WELL, heh, heh...
OW!

SO. THE NEXT TIME I MEET THAT MAN...?
OKAY... OTHER EAR.
I'LL BE READY TO CUT HIM DOWN LIKE A REED.

I *THINK*, ANYWAY. BUT I WONDER IF YOU OR SHIRA ARE GOING TO BEAT ME TO IT...
...*THIS* TIME...

SHIT. NOT *THIS* CRAP AGAIN!
HN?
WHAT DID THOSE GUYS PUT INTO YOUR HEAD?

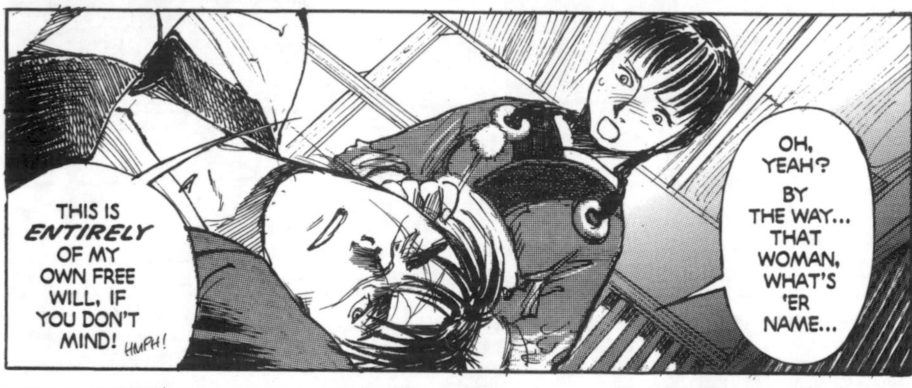
THIS IS *ENTIRELY* OF MY OWN FREE WILL, IF YOU DON'T MIND!
HMPH!
OH, YEAH? BY THE WAY... THAT WOMAN, WHAT'S 'ER NAME...

THAT SCREAM LAST NIGHT...
WHAT THE HELL WAS *THAT* ABOUT?
YOU MEAN *HYAKU-RIN*, RIGHT?
I DON'T REALLY KNOW, EITHER.
DID SHE SAY ANY-THING?
UH-HUH. SHE JUST SAID...

THUD

WELL, WELL, WELL!
NOW AIN'T THIS A SWEET TABLEAU!

HEH HEH HEH
NO, NO-- DON'T GET UP!

CHECK THIS OUT, MANJI!
AARG... BUSTED!

SINCE YOU CAN'T WAIT OUTSIDE, NOT WHEN THEY KNOW WHAT YOU LOOK LIKE...
LET'S WATCH IN COMFORT, HEY? POP THE CORK AND HAVE A FEW SWIGS.

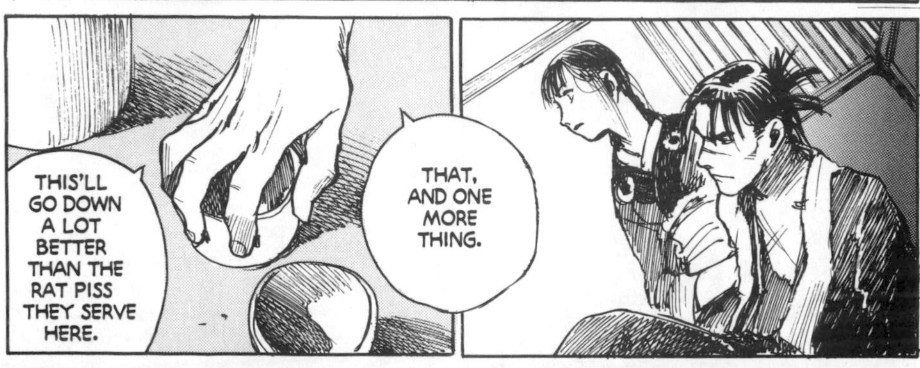
THIS'LL GO DOWN A LOT BETTER THAN THE RAT PISS THEY SERVE HERE.
THAT, AND ONE MORE THING.

I HEARD A PRETTY FUNNY STORY ABOUT ANOTSU.
FROM OUR "FRIEND" INSIDE. FIRST THING THIS MORNING...

HEART OF DARKNESS
Part 3

HE'S IN *DRAG*...?

THAT'S PRETTY OUT THERE.

YEAH... SORTA CREEPY, HUH? BUT IF WE HADN'T HEARD ABOUT IT...
...IT COULD HAVE REALLY THROWN US OFF THE SCENT.

WHEN I READ THAT REPORT ABOUT THOSE KIMONOS AND STUFF...
...I *THOUGHT* SOMETHING WAS KINDA FISHY.

BUT, Y'KNOW, MANJI... IT DOES MAKES THINGS A *WEE* BIT MORE DIFFICULT.

IF THE HEAD OF THEIR WHOLE FREAKIN' SCHOOL IS ACTING THAT WEIRD...
...THERE AIN'T NO TELLIN' WHAT THE REST OF THEM'LL DO.

IF WE JUST GOT FIVE *KENSHI* WALKIN' DOWN THE ROAD... NO PROBLEM, EH?
BUT IF *ALL* OF THEM GET DRESSED UP... THEN HELL, WE MIGHT AS WELL QUIT RIGHT NOW.

HUH?
......
......
C'MON, KIDDO-- NO PROBLEM!
I ONLY SPLASHED IN 'BOUT AS MUCH AS A SPARROW'S PISS, HEY?
AH...? OH...
SPARROW PISS...?
IF HE JUST WANTS TO SHAKE OFF ASSASSINS, THEN SURE, WHY NOT DRAG?
YO, SHIRA.
THAT IDEA DON'T MAKE A GODDAMN LICK OF SENSE.

DE-ONNA: A WOMAN LEAVING EDO. SEE GLOSSARY.

......
......
YOU KNOW... I THINK THAT'S DEFINITELY POSSIBLE.

I MEAN... TWO YEARS AGO...
...WHEN EVERYONE IN THE *MUTENICHI-RYŪ* WAS AMBUSHED AND KILLED?
I SUBMITTED AN OFFICIAL APPEAL TO THE GOVERNMENT JUST TWO DAYS LATER.
BUT FOR SOME REASON...
ONE MONTH WENT BY... THEN TWO MONTHS... AND NO INVESTIGATION WHATSOEVER.

AND LATER, WHEN I WENT TO THE *BUGYŌSHŌ* TO NOTIFY THEM THAT I WOULD BE SEEKING REVENGE...
...I GOT THE TOTAL RUNAROUND, AND THEY NEVER DID GIVE ME PERMISSION, EVEN THOUGH I COMPLIED WITH ALL THE RED TAPE.

THAT'S WHY MY *ADA-UCHI* VENDETTA ISN'T OFFICIALLY REGISTERED BY A *HANTEI-JO*.
AND NORMALLY THESE THINGS AREN'T A PROBLEM... ARE THEY?
SO I'VE WONDER-ED...
...IF THE *ITTŌ-RYŪ* DIDN'T HAVE SOME TIES WITH THE *BAKUFU* BACK THEN... SOMEWHERE BE-HIND THE SCENES. OR IF THE *BAKUFU* ITSELF...

......
......
...PLANNED TO TAKE *ITTŌ-RYŪ* INTO THE FOLD AT SOME POINT, AND WAS DELIBERATELY TURNING A BLIND EYE.
IT'S NOT ***COMPLETELY*** IMPOSSIBLE... IS IT?

YOU SAID YOU'VE SEEN ANOTSU KAGEHISA, RIGHT...?
UM... Y-YES.
JUST THAT DAY TWO YEARS AGO?
NO... ACTUALLY, ONCE MORE-- JUST A FEW DAYS AGO.
WELL? RIGHT?
MANJI... SAVE THE REST OF THAT *SAKE*.
WE'RE GONNA NEED IT REAL SOON...
...*FOR OUR VICTORY CELEBRATION!*

HEART OF DARKNESS
Part 4

THERE.

SOME PICKLES, AND... ANYTHING ELSE?
UM... NO, THAT'S ALL.
THANKS!

?!
LOOK... NOT LIKE I'M SUSPICIOUS OR NOTHING, BUT...

...PRETTY MUCH NO ONE EVER STAYS IN SHINJUKU FOR MORE'N ONE NIGHT.
EVEN FOR *KŌ** AND PLAIN OLD TOURIST STUFF...

*: COMPANIONS GETTING TOGETHER TO VISIT TEMPLES OR TAKE IN THE SIGHTS.

AND ***NO ONE*** EVER COMES DOWN TO THE KITCHEN FOR THEIR FOOD!
OH! OH, REALLY...? I... I'M SORRY!

HA, HA, HA! NOTHING TO BE SORRY ABOUT, GIRL. MORE THAT I'M GRATEFUL, LIKE.
LOOKS LIKE I'LL GET BY WITHOUT SERVICING THOSE MEN OF YOURS.
SPLSSH

EVEN AT THE BEST OF TIMES WE *MESHIMORI-ONNA* DON'T SPEND MUCH TIME IN THE KITCHEN...
...IF YOU KNOW WHAT I MEAN. BUT IN ***THIS*** DUMP THEY EXPECT US TO TAKE CUSTOMERS ON THE SLY.

...?
....

*: FOUR LODGING AREAS BETTER KNOWN AS UNOFFICIAL RED-LIGHT DISTRICTS.
#: ALL RED LIGHT DISTRICTS IN EDO OTHER THAN THE YOSHIWARA.

YOU COME DOWN TO IT, THE *SHI-SHUKU** ARE ALL *OKABASHO#*.
RIGHT, GIRL?

OH... IS THAT SO? I...
WHAT?!

AH... I DIDN'T...
NEITHER OF THEM SAID *ANY-THING* ABOUT...

....
....
...WELL, DEAR, I THOUGHT YOU'D BEEN DOING THE BOTH OF THEM! *AH HA HA!*
WAA HAHA HA!
THERE WASN'T A SINGLE CALL FOR ME, SO I JUST THOUGHT...

WELL, IN THAT CASE, GIRL, THAT MEANS...
...THEY'RE BEHAVIN' THEMSELVES ON ACCOUNT OF YOU? Oh, THOSE TWO POOR GUYS!

AH, WELL, WHATEVER. EVEN IF THEY DID CALL FOR ME...
B-BUT IT ISN'T... I'M N-NOT...
...I'D PROBABLY HAVE TO TURN 'EM DOWN.

DON'T KNOW IF I COULD HANDLE TAKING ON *THOSE* TWO TOUGH BASTARDS!
I... I SEE.
......?
WHY'S THAT?
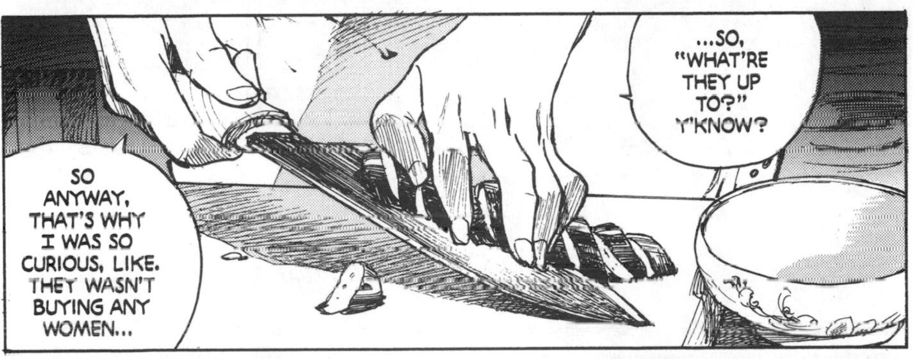
SO ANYWAY, THAT'S WHY I WAS SO CURIOUS, LIKE. THEY WASN'T BUYING ANY WOMEN...
...SO, "WHAT'RE THEY UP TO?" Y'KNOW?

SOME-THING... ***NAUGHTY***, *HMM?*
HELL, NOT THAT IT MATTERS.
NO, I PROMISE WE WON'T CAUSE ANY... ANY...

UM...
CAN I... ASK YOU SOME-THING?

HAVE YOU EVER GONE THROUGH THE KOBOTOKE CHECK-POINT?
HUH?

THE *SEKISHO*? WELL, YEAH. JUST ONCE.
I HEAR LOTS ABOUT IT, THOUGH... ON ACCOUNT OF MY WORK, SEE?

OH. THEN, *UM*, IT'S JUST SORT OF A...A "WHAT IF?" QUES-TION...
BUT...

WHAT IF, JUST FOR EXAMPLE... THERE WAS A GUY WHO LIKE, REALLY LIKED DRESSING UP LIKE A WOMAN OR SOMETHING, AND THAT PERSON...
...WAS LIKE, DRIVEN BY SOME SORT OF, I DUNNO, ***PERVERSE DESIRE*** TO GO THROUGH THE *SEKISHO* ALL DRESSED UP?

I MEAN, HA-HA, OF COURSE THERE WOULDN'T BE ANYTHING ***MORE*** SUSPICIOUS THAN ***THAT***...
...BUT IF HE INSISTED ON DOING IT ANYWAY... IS THERE, LIKE, EVEN ***ONE WAY*** TO PULL IT OFF... YOU THINK?

WELL?
OKAY... WHICH ONE IS IT?
HUH?

JUST, Uh, THEORETICALLY, OKAY?
OH, NO, NO! IT'S NOT ABOUT THEM. I'M JUST MAKING IT UP!
HMM...
THANK GOD, I DIDN'T WANT TO IMAGINE ONE OF THOSE GUYS...

HOW ABOUT IF YOU HAD A CONTACT INSIDE THE GOVERNMENT OR SOMETHING...?
DON'T UNDERESTIMATE THOSE GOVERNMENT GUYS.
CHOK
...I FIGURE ANY OLD SEKISHO WOULD NOTICE SOMETHING LIKE THAT!
DON'T RIGHTLY KNOW WHAT YOU'RE GETTING AT. BUT, GIRL...

I TOLD YOU, GIRL--
--DON'T UNDER-ESTIMATE THEM.
BUT...

THOSE *BANSHI* SAMURAI... IT'S LIKE THEY HAVE A SIXTH SENSE, Y'KNOW?
AND IT'S SHARPER THAN YOU DREAM. THEY SEEM TO SEE RIGHT THROUGH SNEAKS AND TRICKSTERS.

MAYBE BECAUSE OF THAT, A LOT OF *SEKISHO* POSTS GO FROM FATHER TO SON.

AND WHILE THEY MAY SWITCH 'EM FROM *SEKISHO* TO *SEKISHO*, HARDLY NONE OF THEM EVER GET FIRED.

箱根驛

JUST SHOWS HOW MUCH THE *BAKUFU* TRUSTS THEM, RIGHT?

SOME CONNEC-TIONS, A COUPLE LITTLE BRIBES?

HAH!

THAT WOULDN'T HELP ***NOTHIN'***.

YOU'D JUST BE STICKING YOUR HEAD RIGHT IN THE NOOSE.

KTAK

...WHAT ON EARTH IS ANOTSU THINK-ING...?
SHE'S RIGHT. BUT THEN...

TEA, TEA... *HMM.*
FORGOT TO BOIL SOME UP. CAN YOU COME GET IT LATER?

HUH? OH, SURE.

HERE.
GREAT... THANK YOU.

?

SO THAT TALK OF YOURS WAS JUST MAKE BELIEVE, HUH?

BUT THERE *IS* A WAY, I FIGURE. JUST ONE.
A WAY *ANYONE* CAN GET THROUGH A *SEKISHO*.

WELL, THEN... LEMME TELL YA SOME-THING.
TO BE HONEST, IT DEPENDS ON IF THE PARTY IN QUESTON'S GOT THE GUTS FOR IT.

HEART OF DARKNESS
Part 5

HO, GIRL.

YOU WENT TO A LOT OF TROUBLE.
SHOULDA JUST HAD THE *MESHIMORI-ONNA* BRING IT UP.

I DIDN'T HAVE A CHOICE, DID I?
WE DON'T TAKE A STEP OUTSIDE, JUST STARE OUT THE WINDOW ALL DAY LONG.
WOULD YOU RATHER SHE CAME IN AND SAW US DOING THAT?
SHE'D CERTAINLY START WONDERING WHAT WE WERE UP TO.
WHAT'S THE DIF? NOW SHE'S CURIOUS ABOUT THE WEIRDOS WHO COME DOWN FOR THEIR FOOD.
....
WHERE'S MANJI?
OUT BUYING A WHORE.

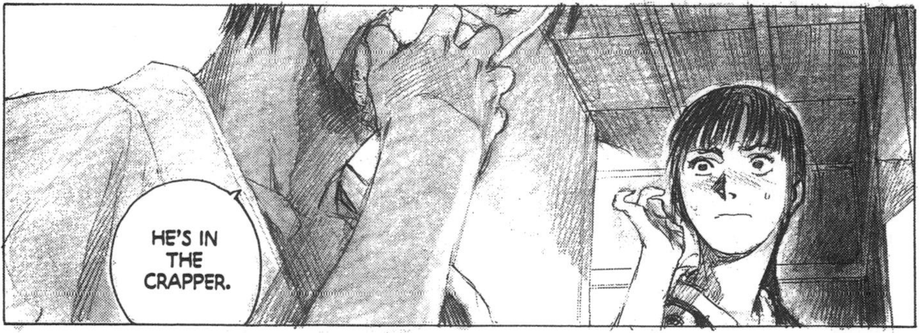

HE'S IN THE CRAPPER.

ANYWAY, I DON'T WANT YOU WANDERING OFF TOO MUCH.
YOUR JOB IS WATCHING FOR ANOTSU, REMEMBER?

OH... RIGHT.

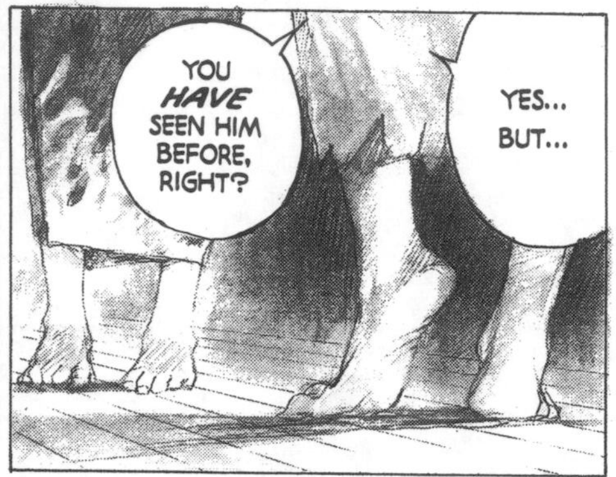
YOU *HAVE* SEEN HIM BEFORE, RIGHT?
YES... BUT...

IF HE'S IN DRAG, THAT COULD MAKE IT KIND OF HARD.
DON'T YOU THINK?
GIMME A BREAK. SO HE'S IN DRAG! IT'S NOT LIKE HIS DICK FELL OFF.

HE CAN'T HIDE THE WAY HE WALKS, HIS BODY LANGUAGE, THAT KIND OF STUFF.
YOU REMEMBER ANY OF THAT?

WELL, *UM*... NO.

IF HE WAS DRESSED LIKE A WOMAN...
...HE COULD LOOK PRETTY ELEGANT.
BUT...

HUH?
...WOULDN'T HE BE ACTING EMBARRASSED? I MEAN, A MAN WHO HEADS A WHOLE SWORD SCHOOL, HIDING HIMSELF LIKE THAT...?

GUESS HE JUST DOESN'T WANT THE HASSLE...
...OF HAVING TO FIGHT A BUNCH OF YOUNG PUNKS OUT TO MAKE A NAME FOR THEMSELVES.

ANYWAY... EVER SINCE THE DAYS OF YAMATO-TAKERU...
...EVERYBODY KNOWS ONLY HEROES AND PERVERTS ARE CRAZY ENOUGH TO DO DRAG.

AND IN THIS BASTARD'S CASE...
...I DECIDE WHICH ONE HE IS!

SO, SHIRA... I GUESS...
...YOU MUST BE PRETTY TOUGH, HUH?
YEAH. I AM.
SO WHAT'S YOUR POINT?
WELL... *UM*... HA, HA!
OH, Y'KNOW...

OH! THAT'S RIGHT!
I NEED TO PICK UP THE TEA!

WHAT? I TOLD YOU TO STAY PUT!
GET IT?

I'LL JUST BE A SEC, HONEST!
ARE YOU LISTENING TO ME? ***HEY!***
USE YOUR DAMN HEAD!

I NEEDED THAT...
WHEWW... THAT WAS SOME SERIOUS LOAD.

DAMN... I'M STARVING.

ARROGANT LITTLE PUNK!
YOU GOT A LOT OF NERVE WITH THIS "HOW DARE YOU?" CRAP!

YOU *CUR!* SAY IT AGAIN!

I *DARE* YOU TO SAY IT AGAIN!

HAH! I'LL SAY IT AS MUCH AS I WANT!

FACT IS, IT'S ALWAYS THE WORTHLESS PUNKS LIKE YOU...

...WHO START WHINING AND SNIVELLING IF YOUR SCABBARDS GET BUMPED A LITTLE IN THE STREET.

WHEN *RŌNIN* START WORRYING ABOUT APPEARANCES, THEY SURE TURN INTO ARROGANT LITTLE SHITS.

THAT WIMPY LOOKIN' SWORD OF YOURS-- WHAT'S THE STORY ON *THAT?*

"WIMPY LOOKING," YOU THINK?

HOW WOULD YOU LIKE TO TEST IT?

WELL, DOG?!
AAH!
H-HE *DREW!*

SHEEE-IT.
A FIGHT, HUH? GIMME A BREAK.

OH-HOH, HE DRAWS HIS SWORD! NOW THERE'S A *REAL* PUNK FOR YOU.

I DON'T LIKE ALL THESE SPECTATORS, BUT SO BE IT.
YOU'LL HAVE ALL ETERNITY TO REFLECT ON YOUR OWN STUPIDITY.

THAT'S GONNA BE *YOUR* JOB, YOU MISERABLE CUR!

"WORDS CAN NEVER HURT YOU," THEY SAY.
BUT WHEN YOU MOCK MY SWORDSMAN-SHIP...

LEADER OF THE *ITTŌ-RYŪ!*
...YOU MOCK THE NAME OF *ANOTSU KAGE-HISA!*

KRASSH!

SHIRA!
WHA-?!

I- I'M SORRY!
IDIOT! I TOLD YOU!

HERE... TAKE A GOOD LOOK...

HUH?! THAT'S HIM? *THE* ANOTSU?!
HUH... HE DON'T LOOK SO TOUGH.
WHAT'S HE DOING HERE?!
WHO? THE *ITTŌ-RYŪ*? IS THAT THE ONE...

......
......
YOU'RE ANOTSU KAGEHISA?!

FAMOUS LITTLE BUGGER, AIN'T HE?
SO HOW ABOUT THIS ALLEGED "ANOTSU" ...?
WELL, GUESS I GOTTA ASK.
THOUGHT SO.
HIM? NO WAY!!
DIDN'T MAKE SENSE TO ANNOUNCE HIS OWN NAME LIKE THAT.

HUH?! *WHY?!*
BUT... WHY DO IT?

WONDER IF THE *RŌNIN* IS A PLANT, TOO?
IT'S PROBABLY ONE OF HIS BODYGUARDS. GOOD SHOW, THOUGH.

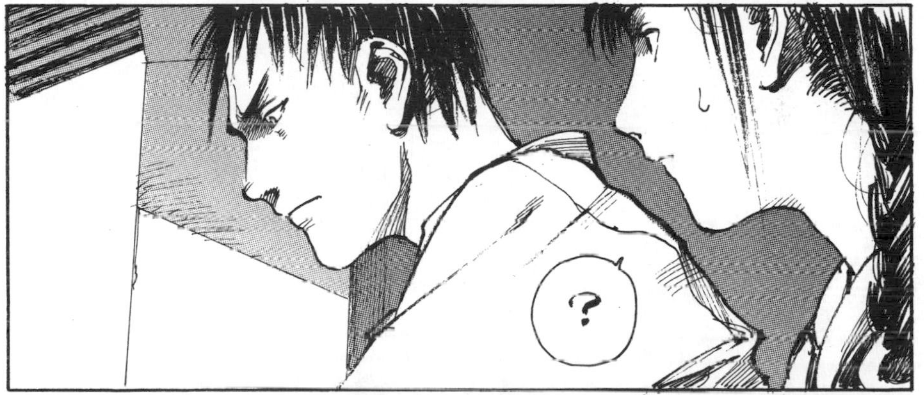
?

LOOK-- OVER THERE. SEE HER?
THAT WOMAN.
HUH?

THE ONE HOLDING THE HAT?
NO! BEHIND HER AND RIGHT!
OH! NOW I SEE HER!

SEE? SHE'S JUST WALKING AWAY, TOTALLY IGNORING THE UPROAR.
GOT SOME HEIGHT ON HER, TOO... FOR A BROAD.
Hmmm

YES, I DO SEEM TO REMEMBER HIM BEING AT LEAST THAT TALL, BUT...BUT...
...THOSE SURE AREN'T A GUY'S HIPS.
AND IF HER TITS AND ASS ARE ALL PADDING?

MMM... YEAH.
AAH! SHE'S GETTING AWAY!

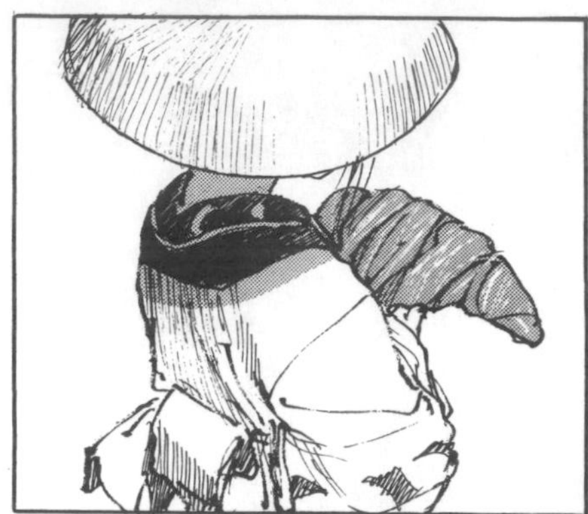

!

WAIT! THAT THING!
THAT AXE!

ANOTSU HAD A WEAPON JUST LIKE IT!
SEE? ALL WRAPPED UP IN CLOTH!

--THERE'S NO WAY A WOMAN COULD CARRY IT LIKE THAT.
IT WEIGHS A TON--
BUT, IF THAT'S NOT A SHE...
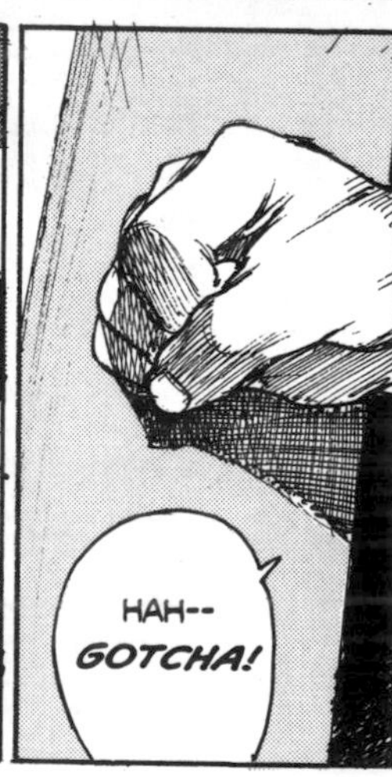
HAH-- GOTCHA!

TOO BAD FOR THE GUYS TROLLING IN THE OTHER RIVER...

...BUT THE ONE WITH THE FISH WINS, BY GOD!

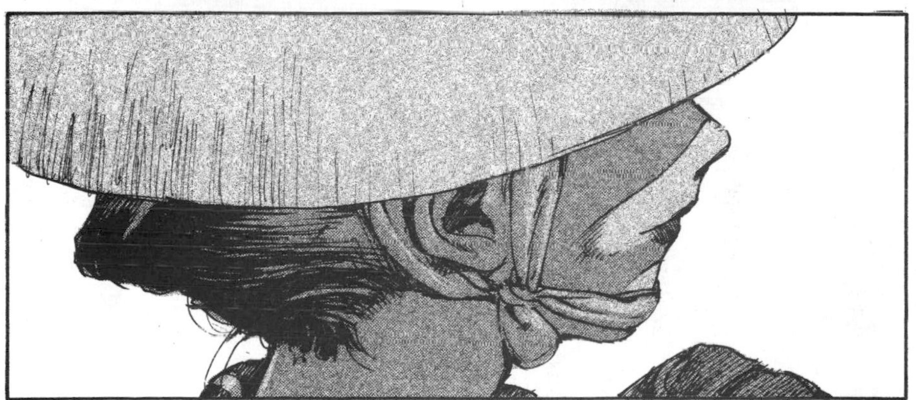

旅籠
THAT'S ANOTSU?
WHAT THE HELL KINDA "DRAG" IS THAT?

WHAT A MESS. THREE OF US HERE...
...AND ONLY ONE OF US KNOWS WHAT HE LOOKS LIKE. THIS SUCKS.

SHOULD I GO GET RIN? NAW... THERE'S NO GUARANTEE THEY'LL BE AT THIS LONG ENOUGH.

ANOTSU'S FACE.
I GOT A FEELING I HEARD SOMETHING ONCE, SOMEWHERE. WHERE THE HELL ***WAS*** THAT...?

HE... HE DIDN'T GIVE ME A NAME...

...BUT H-HE WAS A YOUNG SAMURAI, SIR!

W-WITH NARROW EYES AND LONG HAIR...

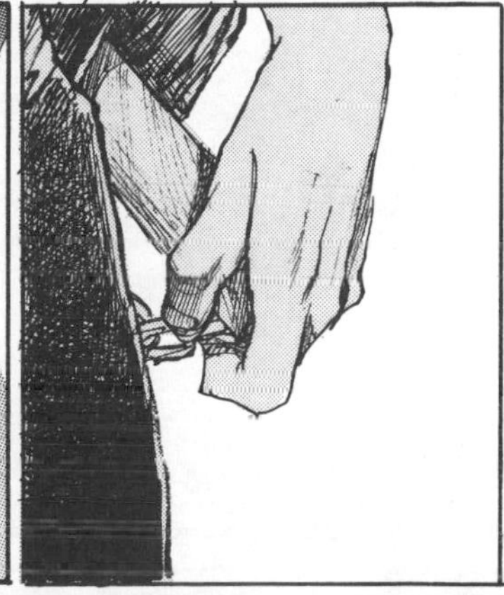

WELL, HE CAN'T BE STRONGER THAN *HER*...

...CAN HE?

.....
.....

CAN IT *REALLY* BE HIM...?
...SUCH THIN ANKLES!

LOOKING FROM THIS CLOSE UP...
UH-OH.

BUT THEN...
...TO CARRY THAT AXE...

WE'VE WALKED FOUR AND A HALF *RI*.
HUH?

SO, WHA-- OH?!
NO! W-WAIT A SEC!

?!
QUIET DOWN, KID!
LOOK, SHIRA.
WE CAN'T JUST... CUT HIM DOWN FROM BE-HIND!
AT LEAST WAIT UNTIL I'VE SEEN HIS FACE!

YOU'RE HAVING SECOND THOUGHTS NOW?!
WHY?

WELL, UM... JUST LOOK.
NO BODY-GUARDS, NOTHING.

AS SOON AS HE LOOKS BACK AT US, I'LL KNOW. AND THEN...
LET'S GET CLOSER AND TALK TO HIM.
......
......
WELL, SHIT!

SO HOW'RE YA GONNA DO IT?
OH, UH... MAYBE...
SOMETHING LIKE-- "MA'AM, YOU DROPPED SOME-THING!"

kchink

THANK YOU KINDLY, YA BASTARD!

SO YOU WANT TO DO IT *HERE*, HUH?

?!

Uh... EXCUSE ME, MA'AM?! YOU DROPPED SOME-THING!
I THINK IT'S YOUR MONEY POUCH!

.....
...?
TH-THEY STOPPED!
NOW...?

YOU WANT ME TO TEACH YOU SOME MANNERS WITH THE EDGE OF MY SWORD?!

WE SAID YA DROPPED SOME-THING!

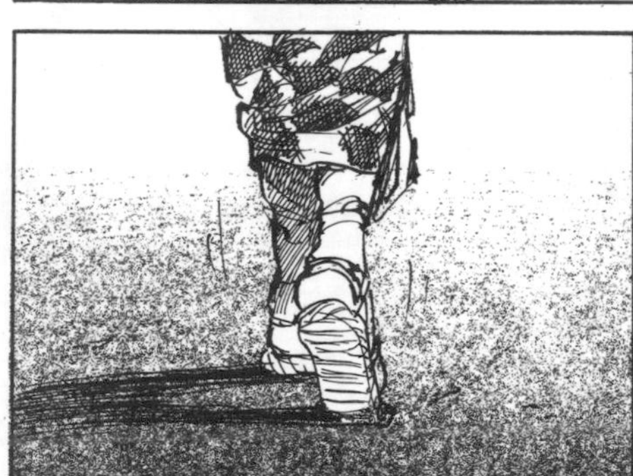

HEY.

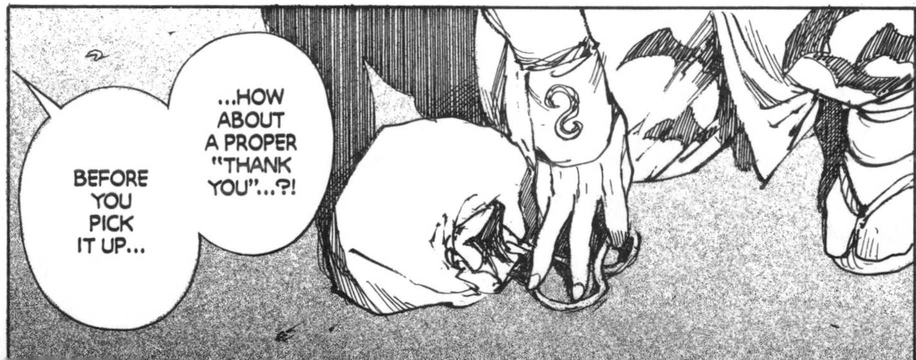
BEFORE YOU PICK IT UP...
...HOW ABOUT A PROPER "THANK YOU"...?!

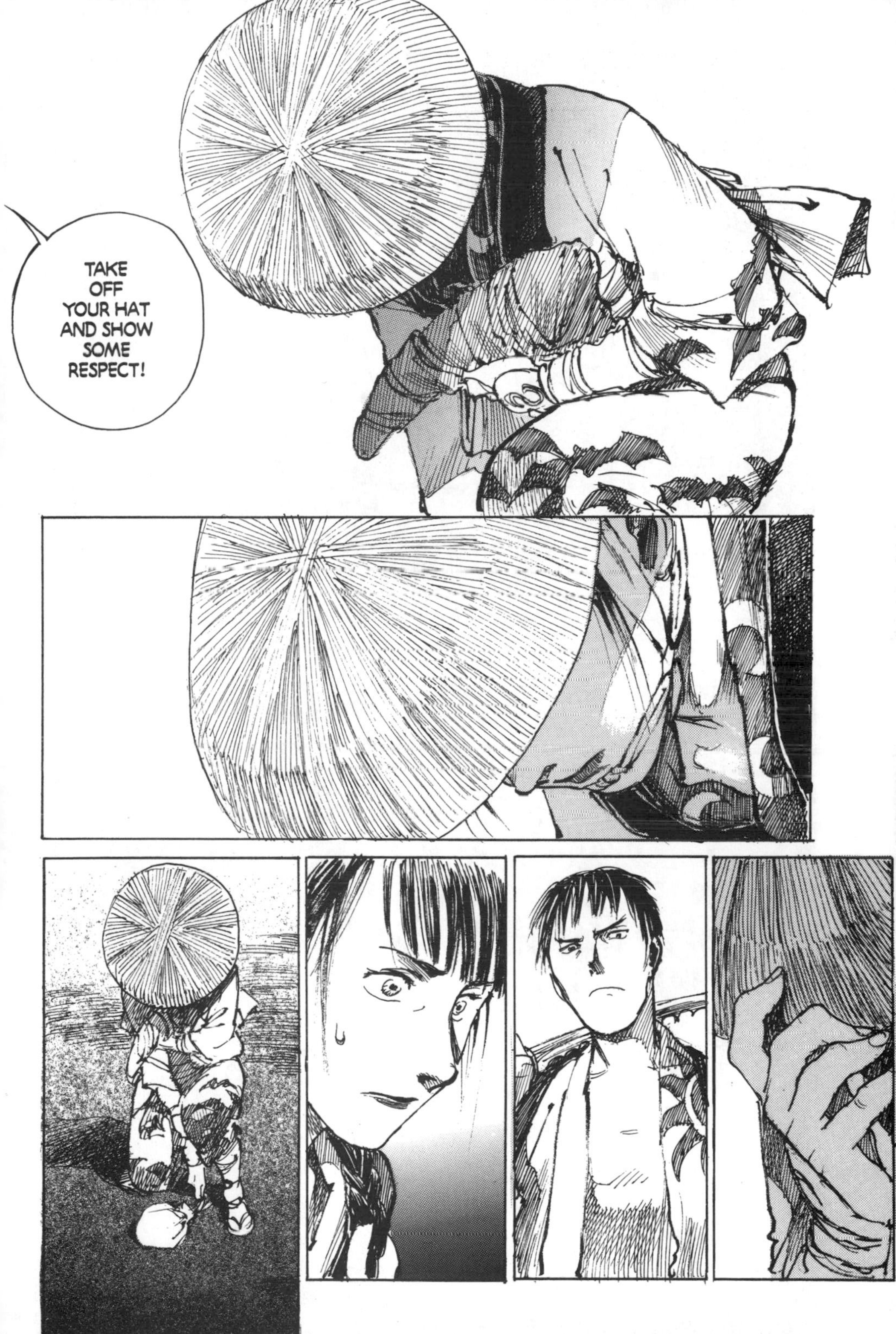
TAKE OFF YOUR HAT AND SHOW SOME RESPECT!

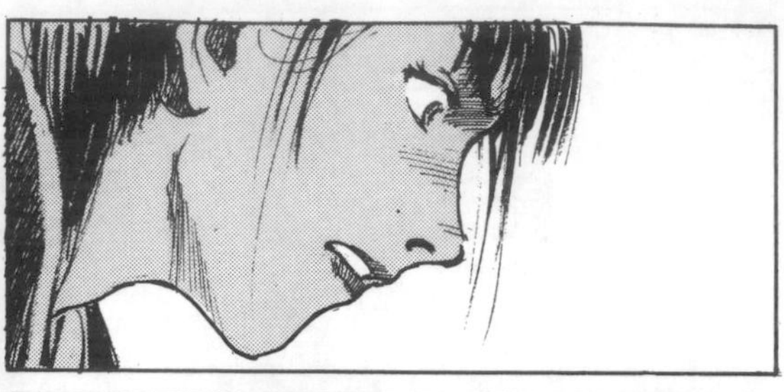

AH...?!

DON'T
YOU
GOT ANY
EARS,
YOU
FRIGGIN'
BITCH?!

KTONK

"KTONK"...?!

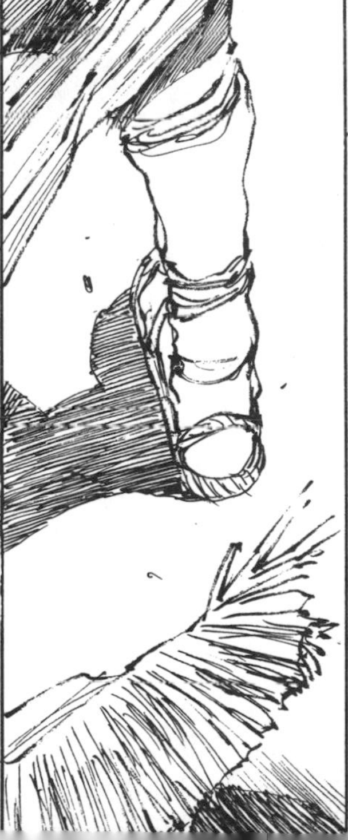

......
......

HEY!
YOU AIN'T NO DUDE!
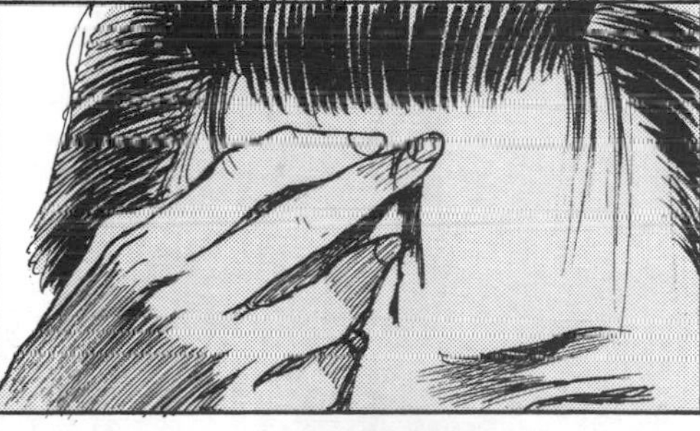

!

WHAT AN AWFUL THING TO DO!
MY FACE IS MY *LIVELIHOOD*, SIR!

WHATEVER MADE YOU THINK THAT I WAS A MAN?
AND I MUST CONFESS TO BEING SOMEWHAT CURIOUS ABOUT YOUR COMMENT.

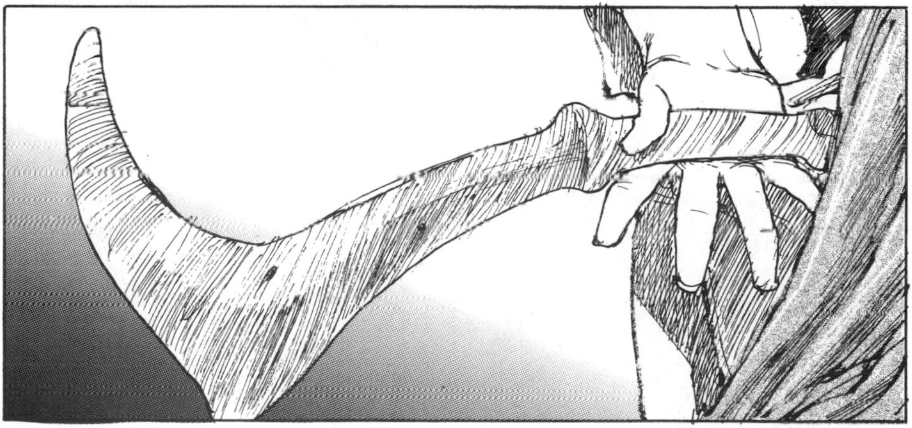

...?!
WOOD...?

WELL, SHIT. SHIT!
WHAT A FRIGGIN' *JOKE!*
BUT I AIN'T LAUGHIN'.
WHAT KIND OF WHINY LITTLE SNOT YOU GOT FOR A BOSS?
HE REALLY THAT SCARED OF US OTHER *KENSHI*?
WETTING HIS PANTS, IS HE? ***HUH?!***

IS
HE?!
KTONK

!

THE FRIENDS OF THE SPY?
SO IT *IS* YOU, IS IT?

YOUR AVERAGE *KENSHI* WOULD HAVE BEEN THROWN OFF BY THAT DISTURBANCE BACK IN TOWN.
THANK YOU. THAT'S ALL I NEEDED TO SEE, TO KNOW I'M RIGHT.

ONLY A HANDFUL OF PEOPLE BESIDE OUR LEADER KNOW ABOUT THIS SCHEME.
YET APPARENTLY IT NEVER OCCURRED TO YOU TO QUESTION YOUR AGENT'S INFORMATION.

OF COURSE, BY NOW YOUR SPY MAY HAVE CAUGHT ON.
THE GARMENTS I CHANGED OUT OF AT THE *DŌJŌ* RESIDENCE WILL STILL SMELL OF A WOMAN, AFTER ALL.

SO *THAT* WAS IT-- THEY WERE TRYING TO SMOKE OUT THE MOLE AS WELL.
TWO BIRDS WITH ONE STONE!

HUH.

WELL, I'LL BE DIPPED IN DOGSHIT. HE REALLY THOUGHT THIS ONE THROUGH, DIDN'T HE?
AIN'T HE A CLEVER L'IL DICKENS!

HE FIGURED WE'D BE LAYING FOR HIM AT THE *SHI-SHUKU*...
...AND PLANNED TO DO US IN, WITH YOU AS THE LURE. RIGHT?

NOT QUITE. FIRST...

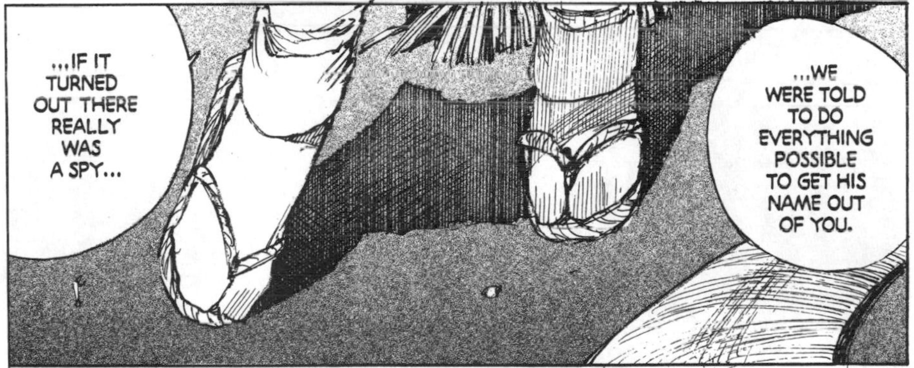

...WE WERE TOLD TO DO EVERYTHING POSSIBLE TO GET HIS NAME OUT OF YOU.
...IF IT TURNED OUT THERE REALLY WAS A SPY...
!

...HIRED AS *BAIT*, NOTHING MORE.
ME? HA HA! GOOD SIR, I'M JUST AN ORDINARY GEISHA...

OH, YEAH? WHO'S GONNA GET IT OUT OF US, AND HOW?!
YOU SURE AS HELL AIN'T!
I MEAN, GIMME A BREAK!

MY ROLE IN THIS WAS TO KEEP YOU OCCUPIED...
...UNTIL THE BOYS FROM *ITTŌ-RYŪ* ARRIVED.

SEE...?

I MUST SAY I'M QUITE RELIEVED THEY'RE FINALLY HERE...

HEART OF DARKNESS
Part 6

?!
IS THAT YOU, SAIKAYA? IT'S BEEN A WHILE!
HA HA... SO IT HAS! FANCY MEETING YOU HERE, O-SEI!
HAVEN'T SEEN YOU SINCE YOU WERE WORKING AT THAT HIKOJU PLACE. HOW'S IT GOING?

QUITE WELL, THANK YOU.
AND YOU...? HOW'S BUSINESS?

OH, SO-SO.
BUT YOU KNOW WHAT THEY SAY--WHEN THE DOCTOR AND THE DRUGGIST MAKE MONEY, THEY'RE THE ONLY HAPPY ONES.

SO I COULD BE *HAPPIER*, IF YOU CATCH MY DRIFT ...EH?

ENDS UP I SPEND MOST OF MY TIME HAVING *THIS* SORT OF FUN INSTEAD...
...IF YOU KNOW WHAT I MEAN.

WHOO
OOMPH!

DO YOU HAVE ANYTHING TO STOP BLEED-ING?

HERE YOU GO.
YOU BET. AND SO... WHAT SHALL WE DO ABOUT THESE FOLKS ANNOYING YOU?

I'VE DONE MY PART-- THE REST IS NONE OF MY BUSINESS.
THAT'S UP TO YOU.
FAIR ENOUGH, MY DEAR.

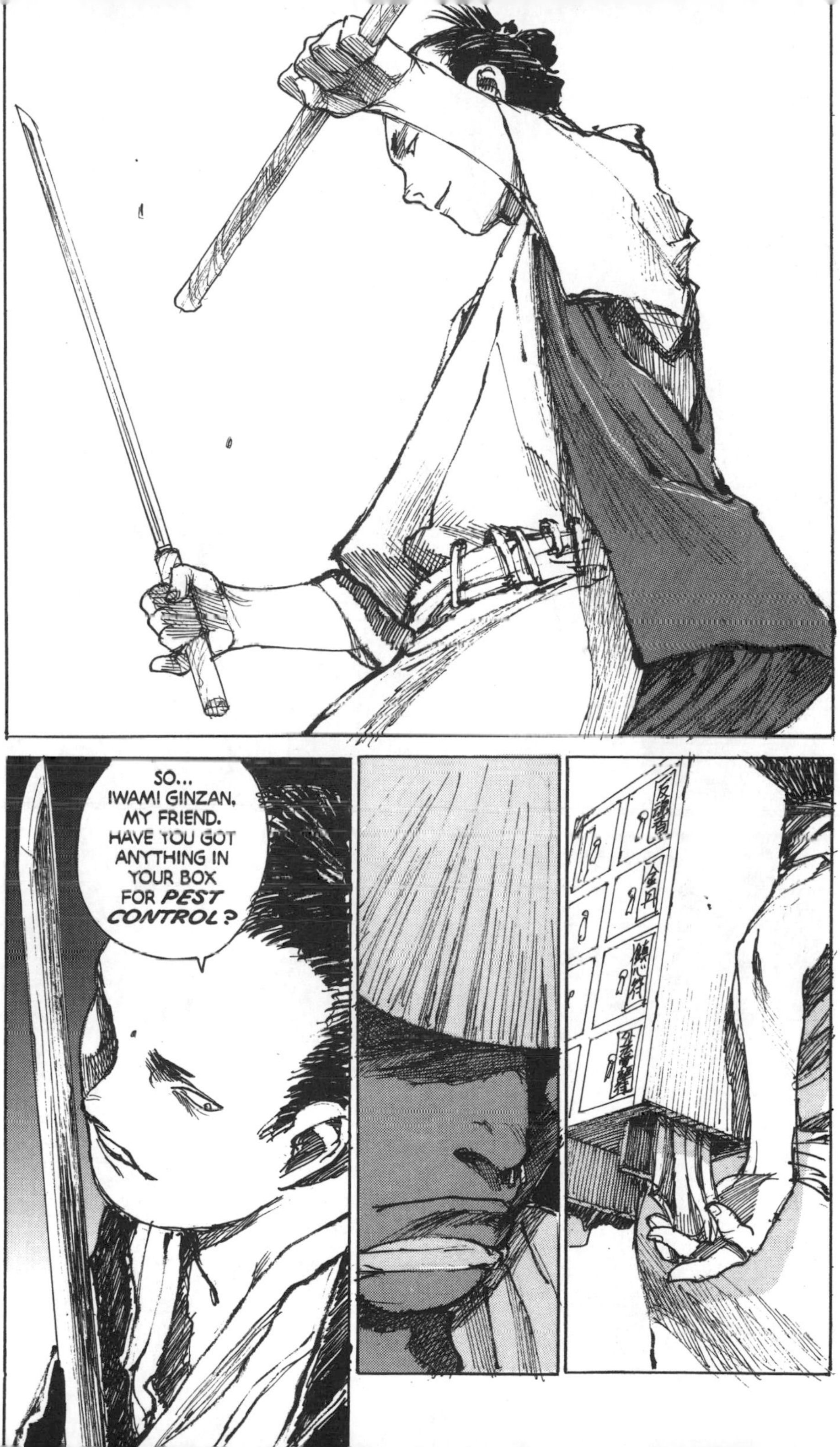

SO... IWAMI GINZAN, MY FRIEND. HAVE YOU GOT ANYTHING IN YOUR BOX FOR ***PEST CONTROL***?

......
......

WELL, *SHIT*.

ONE AND A HALF RYŌ EACH...
...SO TWO OF 'EM MAKES THREE RYŌ.
AND THE BITCH AIN'T WORTH SQUAT.

AND HERE I WAS EXPECTING A GOOD *THIRTY RYŌ* FOR ANOTSU.
HARDLY SEEMS FAIR, DO IT?
WELL, IF THAT'S THE WAY WE'RE GONNA PLAY IT, THEN LISTEN UP, RIN!
?
WHAT-EVER HAPPENS, *DON'T* DRAW YOUR SWORD!
EVERY ONE OF THESE GUYS...
...IS *MY* TOY TO PLAY WITH!

??
I DON'T UNDER-STAND. WH-
SHUDDUP!
ALL YOU NEED TO KNOW IS THAT IF YOU BUTT IN, I'LL KILL *YOU*, TOO.

HA HA... WHY, *THANK YOU*, SIR. TO BE SO GROSSLY UNDER-ESTIMATED...

...IS NOT MERELY IMPRESSIVE, BUT DOWNRIGHT *ASTONISH-ING!*
AND WHAT EXACTLY DO YOU PLAN TO DO WITH THAT... *THING?*

YOU'RE GOING TO DUEL ME WITH A *SAW?* WHAT ARE YOU-- A CARPENTER?! *HA HA!*

I SPEND ALL THIS TIME WAITING, AND THEN HAUL MY BUTT ALL THE WAY OUT HERE...
...AND ALL I FIND IS SOME WHORE-HOUSE SKANK?

IF I'D KNOWN *THAT*, I SURE AS HELL WOULDN'T BE WASTING MY TIME OUT HERE IN THE BUSH, GETTIN' MOSQUITO BITES ON MY ASS.

TO HELL WITH *THIS* SHIT! I'M GOING RIGHT BACK TO EDO TO FIND ME SOME *DECENT* BITCHES TO RAPE.

TOO BAD, THOUGH...

...I'D LOVE TO SLICE YOU OPEN AND PITCH YOUR STINKIN' GUTS INTO THE KANDAGAWA RIVER!
THEN I'D WATCH THE FISH FEED ON 'EM WHILE I KICKED BACK AND SIPPED A LITTLE BREW!

......
......

ALL... IS... VANITY...
......
......
......

YO. BUDDY.
GOT A QUESTION FOR YA.

??

TRUTH BE TOLD, I AIN'T NEVER SEEN ANOTSU BEFORE.
TODAY'S THE FIRST TIME. BUT LIKE... HOW SHOULD I PUT IT...?

I KNOW EVERY WAR STORY GETS BIGGER IN THE TELLING, BUT ***SHIT!***
IF A WIMP LIKE THAT CAN DO IT, THEN MAN, WHAT A CUSHY GIG, EH? RUNNING YOUR OWN SWORD SCHOOL, I MEAN.
SO? WHAT DO ***YOU*** THINK, MISTER *RŌNIN*...?
I DUNNO...
NO ***REAL*** REASON TO DOUBT HIM, I GUESS.
MAYBE THE CREDIT BELONGS TO YOUR SWORD ARM.
OH YEAH...?!

MUCH OBLIGED FOR THE KIND WORDS, STRANGER!
IN THAT CASE... I'LL JUST LEAVE IT AT THAT.

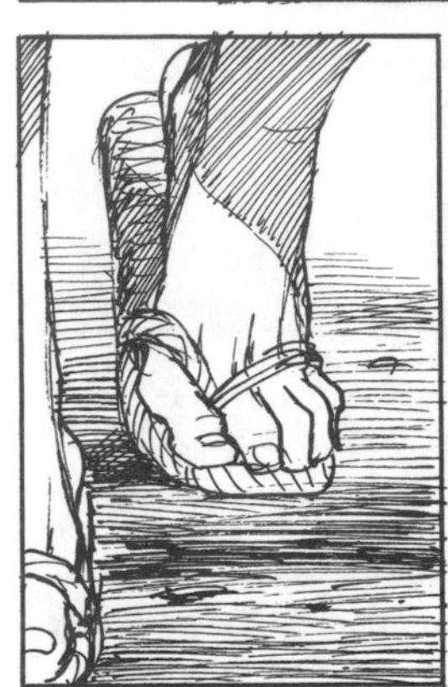

SEE YA.

HANG IN THERE!

......
......

......
......

SHKK

FORGIVE ME!

SCSSH
CHOK

SKSSH HH

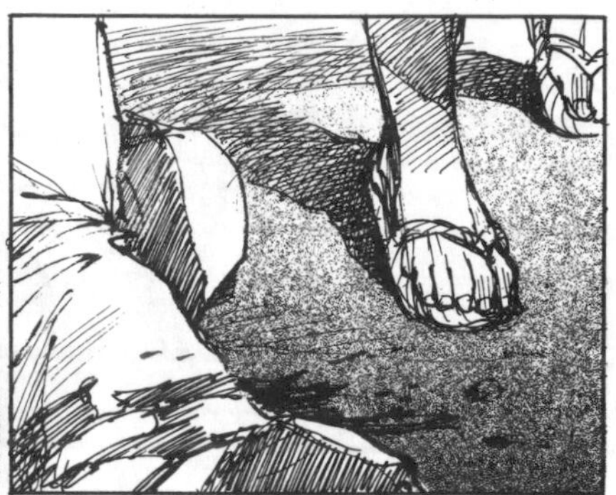

OH, WELL.
WHERE'D THE *REAL* ONE GO, I WONDER?

GCHAK
......
......
...?
AH...
AAAGH!

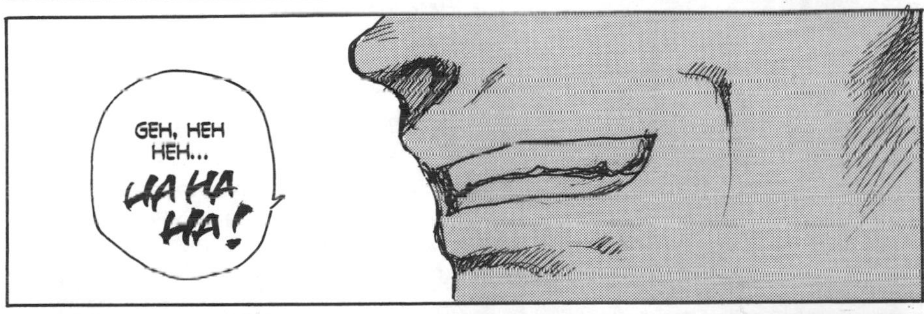
GEH, HEH HEH... HA HA HA!

I... I DON'T BELIEVE IT!

.....
.....

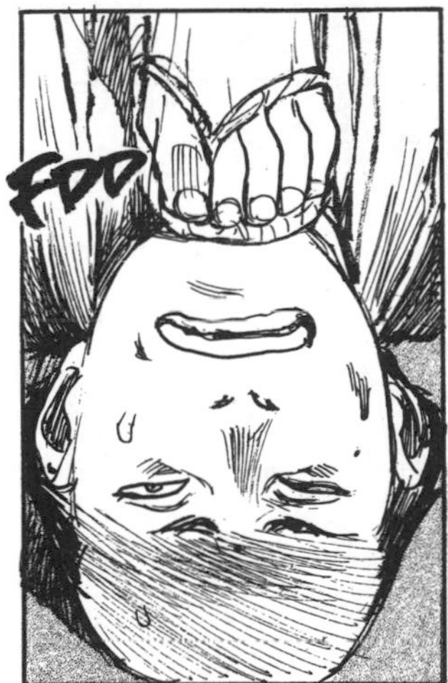
FDD

SHIRA PUSHED ME AND I WENT FLYING...
AND BY THE TIME I GOT UP AND TURNED AROUND...

SO... DO YOU WANNA KNOW?

HNNG... AAG...

...THAT GUY'S LEG W-WAS ALREADY IN THE AIR...!

I ASKED, "DO YOU WANNA KNOW"...?
I DIDN'T ASK IF YOU WANTED TO *DIE*, ASSHOLE.
DAMN YOU! IF YOU'RE GONNA KILL ME, THEN *KILL ME!*

"WHAT," YOU SAY?!

K-KNOW W-WHAT...?

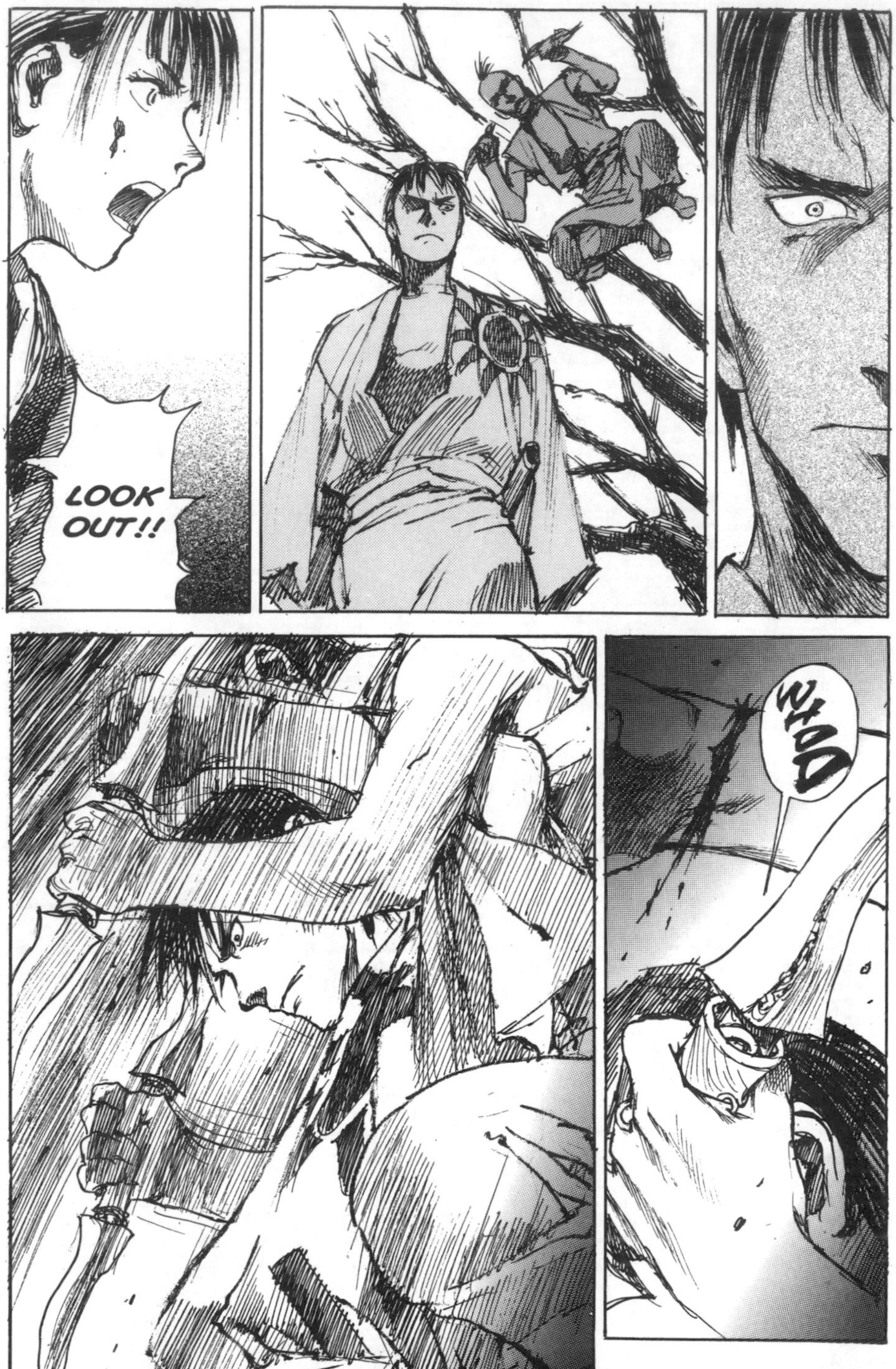

LOOK OUT!!

HHNG!!
HYAAH!
FWAP

WHRAK

GMPH

NOW IT'S ALL *PLAY TIME!*
AND *NOBODY* RUINS MY FUN!
HEH, HEH, HEH...

SHIRA! ARE YOU--
I SAID *BUTT OUT,* GIRL!

HEART OF DARKNESS
Part 7

BWAHAW HAW HAW!

IT'S *ME.* *I'M* THE GUY THAT'S GOT A RIGHT TO BE ANGRY.
YOU GOT IT *BACK-WARDS*, YOU DUMB SHIT.

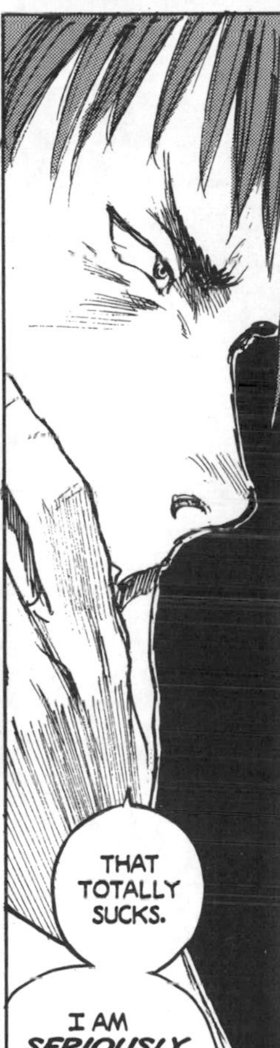
THAT TOTALLY SUCKS.

WHAT PISSES ME OFF MOST...
...IS THAT NOW HYAKURIN OR THAT ASSHOLE GIICHI ARE GONNA SNAG THE GRAND PRIZE.

I AM *SERIOUSLY* HACKED OFF! SO...*NOW* WHAT TO DO...?

......?
NOW I GET IT!

EVEN IF THE KŌSHŪ BYWAY HERE WAS A BUST...
...ANOTSU MAY HAVE RUN INTO HYAKURIN AND THE OTHERS ON THE ROADS *THEY* WERE WATCHING.

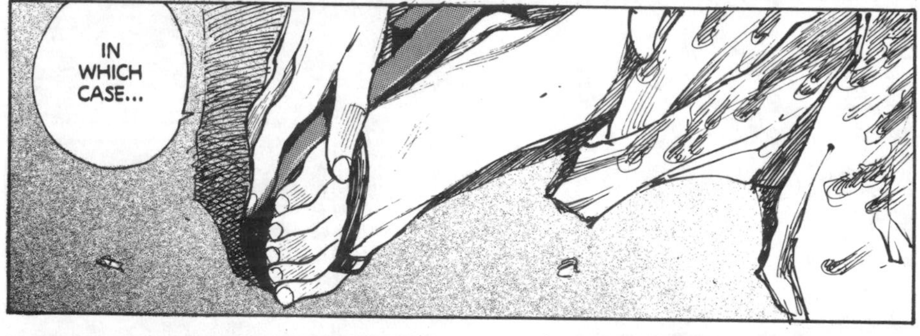
IN WHICH CASE...

HUAAA!

COME AND GET IT!

HO! READY FOR MORE, EH?
COOL.

THAP
HNG!

RYAA!
CHOK

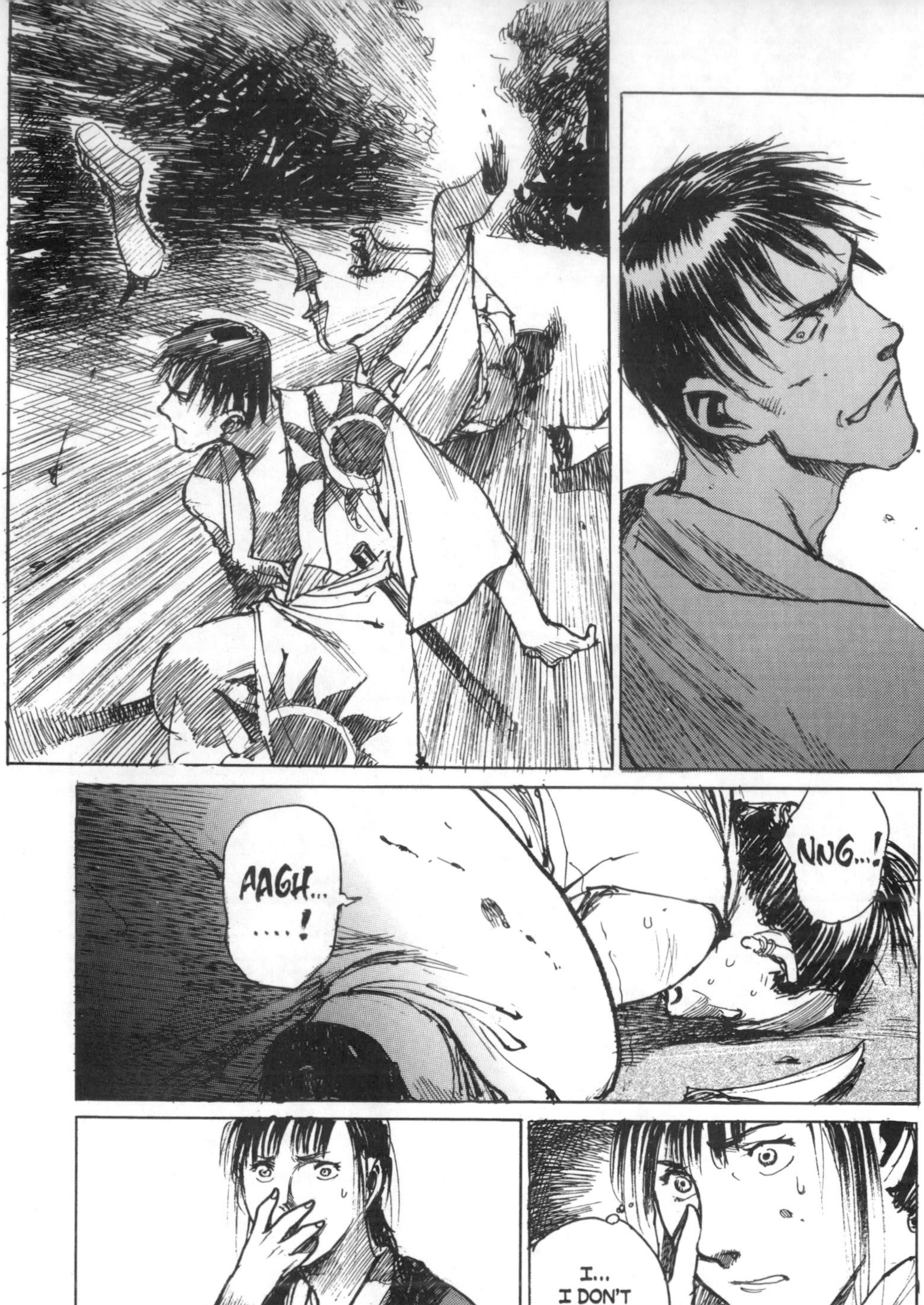

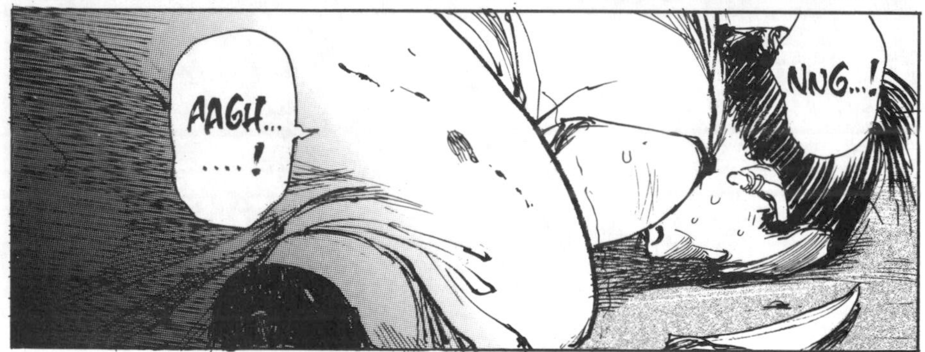
NNG...!
AAGH... ....!

I... I DON'T BELIEVE IT!

BEFORE, AND NOW THIS TIME, TOO...

HE'S *AIMING* FOR THEIR LEGS, RIGHT FROM THE VERY BEGINNING!

......

......!

STARTING FROM THAT POSITION...TO BE ABLE TO MOVE TO MAKE THAT SORT OF CUT... *INCREDI-BLE!*

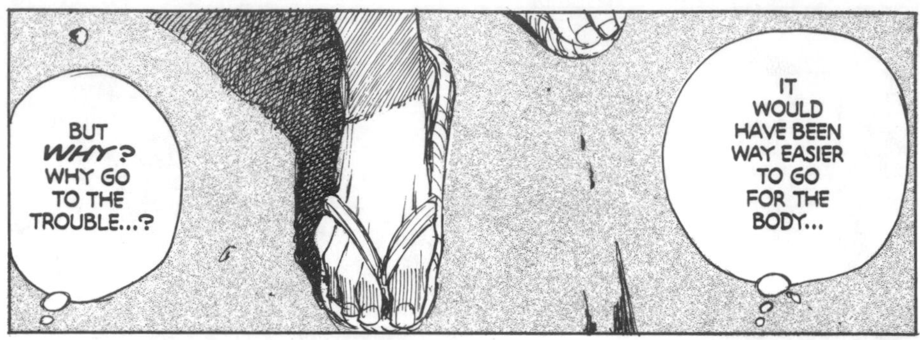
IT WOULD HAVE BEEN WAY EASIER TO GO FOR THE BODY...
BUT *WHY*? WHY GO TO THE TROUBLE...?

LOOKIN' GOOD, PAL.

......
......

BOTH YOUR LEGS WHACKED OFF...
...AND YOU DON'T EVEN WHIMPER. YOU GOT *SERIOUS* BALLS.

CHOK

NNG AAH!
AW, MAN... DON'T DISAPPOINT ME *NOW!*

WELL, WHATEVER.
EVERYTHING'S READY, ANYWAY.

I'D LOVE TO SPEND SOME QUALITY TIME WITH YOU GUYS.

BUT THIS HERE BEING A *MAIN ROAD* AND ALL, GUESS I'D BETTER GET DOWN TO BUSINESS.

IN WHICH CASE...

...FOR *YOU*, THIS'LL HAVE TO DO!

?!

NNN GHH!
AAH...!

HEH... I'VE BEEN WANTIN' TO DO THIS FROM THE SECOND I SAW YOU.
AAAGH!

....!

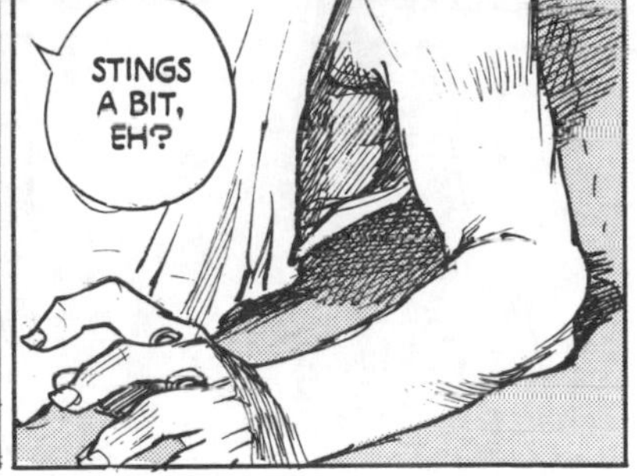
STINGS A BIT, EH?

MMGH!

SHRIKK
OOPS.

BWA HAW HAW HAW!
AH, WELL. GUESS I'LL LET YOU OFF EASY.

SPSSH

SPLTT
!

CLIP IT ON YOUR EAR OR NOSE, WHAT-EVER.
HE SURE DON'T NEED IT NO MORE.

HERE! CATCH!

SH...

SHIT...!
WHO? *ME?* YOU MEAN *ME?*

AW, FORGET IT. NOW... WE WERE TALKING, WEREN'T WE? SO NOW I'LL TELL YOU...
...WHAT YOU WERE ASKING ABOUT BEFORE!

??
YOU SAID SOMETHING LIKE... "WHAT THE HELL ARE YOU GONNA DO...
...WITH A *SAW?*"
WELL... FIRST, I'M GONNA DO *THIS*.
GSHK

AAG! AAHG! AAHNG!

MAN, THE GUY SQUAWLS ABOUT EVERY LITTLE SCRATCH. AIN'T YOU SUPPOSED TO BE A DOCTOR OR A DRUGGIST OR SOMETHING? PUSSY!

HELL, IT SHOULDN'T EVEN HURT THAT MUCH YET.
WITH A NICE CLEAN WOUND WITH A SHARP SWORD...

...SHOULD TAKE A LITTLE WHILE BEFORE YOU EVEN FEEL IT.

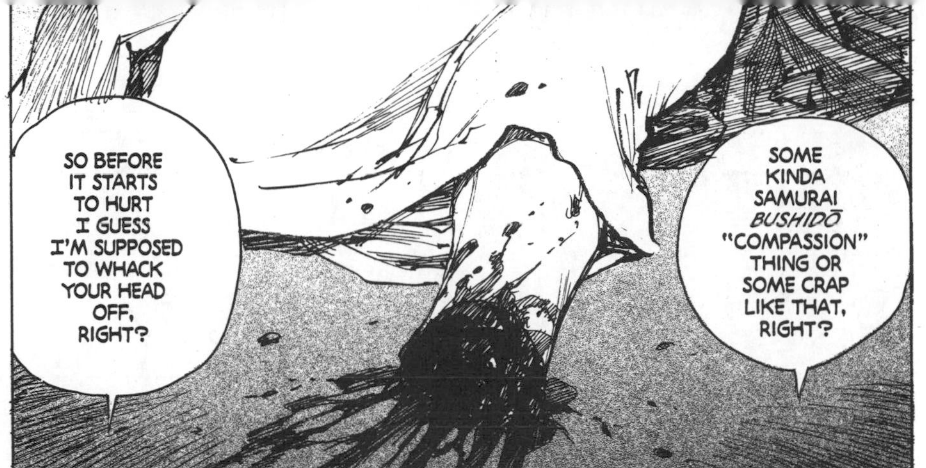
SOME KINDA SAMURAI *BUSHIDŌ* "COMPASSION" THING OR SOME CRAP LIKE THAT, RIGHT?
SO BEFORE IT STARTS TO HURT I GUESS I'M SUPPOSED TO WHACK YOUR HEAD OFF, RIGHT?

BESIDES, I'M STILL PISSED AT YOU FOR WASTING MY GODDAMN TIME.
WELL, SORRY, PAL. THAT SHIT DON'T CUT ANY ICE WITH ME.

AND SO-- *HMM*...

YOU'RE ANGRY TOO... RIGHT?
Eh... AH... WELL...
RIGHT, LITTLE LADY...?

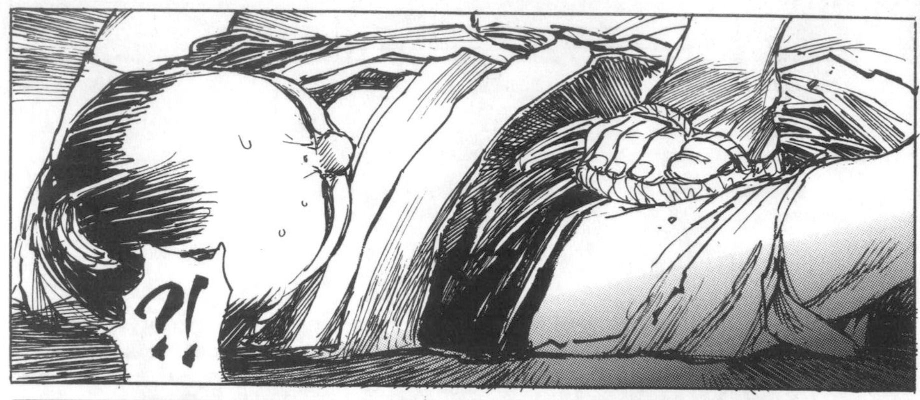
?!

RIGHT ABOUT *HERE*, EH?

HE WOULDN'T ...?

ONE, TWO...
GRCCH
!!
NNG...

N-NO! WAIT! STOP!!

AAAGAHH!

OH SHIT! IT HURTS! AAGHH! YOU BASTARD!!
REALLY?! EXCELLENT! IN FACT, PERFECT!

GOOD LUCK FOR ME THAT I LEFT THE REAL SCREAMER FOR LAST!
BWA HAW HAW HAW HAW HAW!

GGGGH
GRGGH

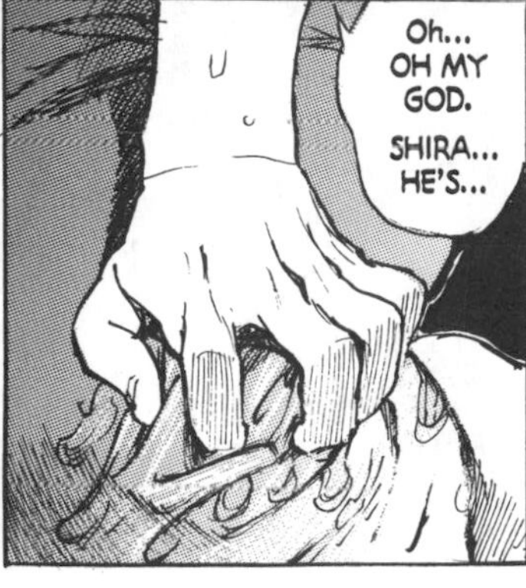
Oh... OH MY GOD. SHIRA... HE'S...

NNNG
FDD
AAH!
K-KILL ME!! PLEASE!! WHY D-DON'T YOU JUST KILL ME?!

HUH? C'MON, DON'T BE A QUITTER!
GRCCCH
"NEVER SAY DIE," RIGHT? HEH, HEH!
I HAVEN'T POLISHED IT UP LATELY, SO IT DOESN'T CUT AS GOOD AS IT COULD, BUT HEY...
...IT'LL ALL BE OVER IN A MINUTE, ANYWAY.

......
......
...!

THIS... IS THIS ANY WAY TO KILL...?

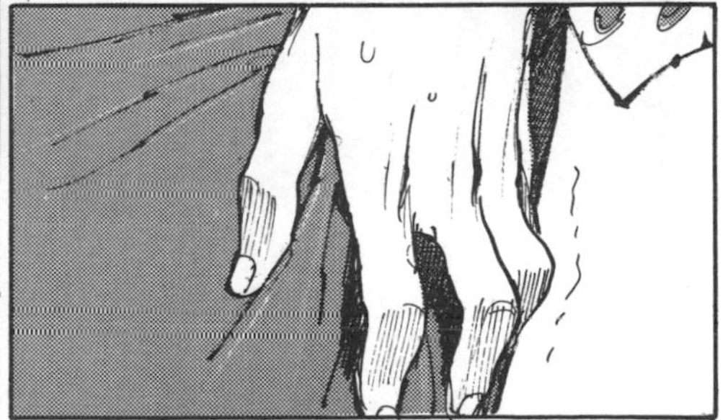

THAT'S WHAT SHIRA SAID.
"*I'M* THE GUY THAT'S GOT A RIGHT TO BE ANGRY."

IS THIS WHY I'M SO WEAK? BECAUSE I DON'T FEEL THE WAY HE DOES?
I KNEW IT MIGHT HAPPEN THAT WAY, SO SURE, I WAS STILL A LITTLE ANGRY. BUT...
WE SPENT TWO DAYS WAITING, ALL THREE OF US, AND ANOTSU TOOK ANOTHER ROUTE.
OKAY.

NO. WHAT-EVER IT IS THAT MAKES SHIRA STRONG...
...IT'S *TOTALLY* DIFFERENT FROM THE SORT OF STRENGTH MANJI HAS.

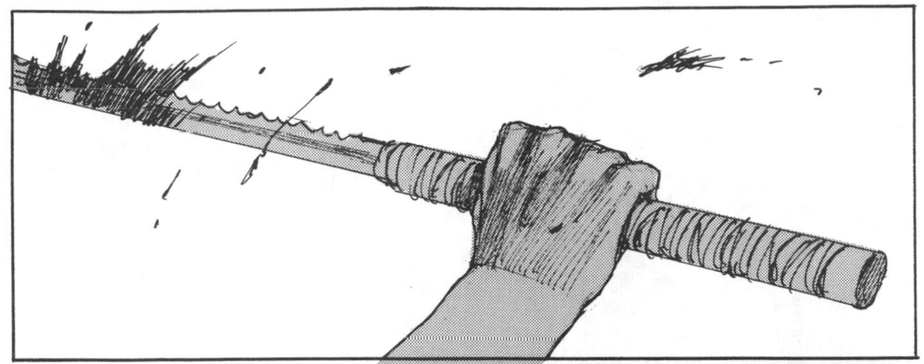

THD

NNK.
NNG... AHH...

Y-YOU ROTTEN B... BASTARD...

CHCHOK

HUHN.

DIDN'T BEG FOR HIS LIFE.
WELL, HELL. THAT'S PRETTY GOOD.

SHIRA...

BUTT OUT.

EH? BUT...

JUST KEEP YOUR MOUTH SHUT!

THERE'S STILL ONE LEFT. THE WORST ONE OF ALL.

......
...!

OH, NO... YOU WOULDN'T...

SKSSH

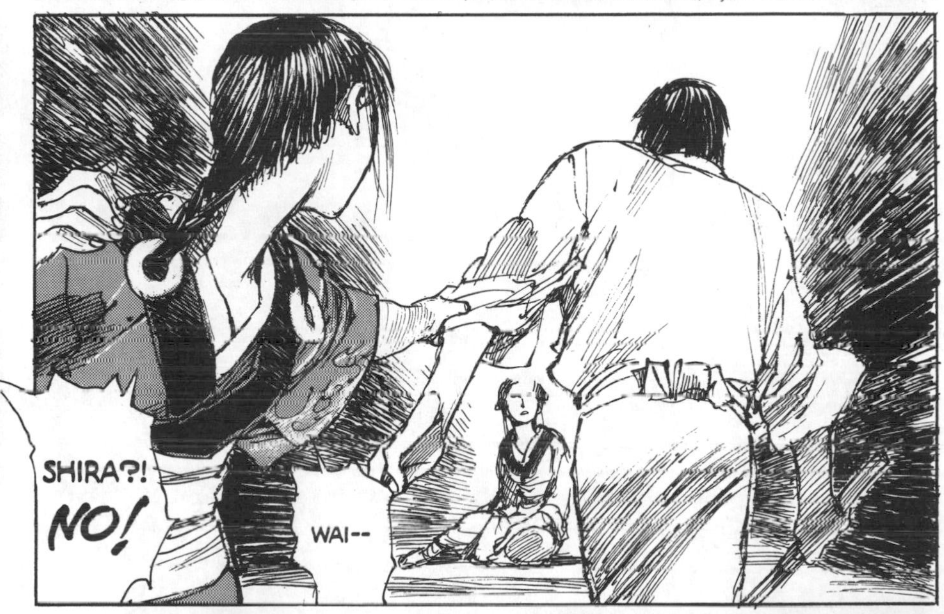
SHIRA?!
NO!
WAI--

OH...?!

OH, NO...
NO!

WHSSH

HEART OF DARKNESS
Part 8

WHOA... BUMMER. *BIG* TIME.

MAJOR, *MAJOR* DRAG!

?

EEK!
EEK!
EEEK!
WELL, THEY'RE *REAL*.

Hmph.

WHAK

SO... TELL ME, SHINRIJI DEAR.
IF YOU DON'T MIND...
WHEN A TOUGH GUY WHO RUNS A KICK-ASS SWORD SCHOOL DECIDES TO QUEER OUT AND PLAY DRAG QUEEN, YOU FIGURE IT'S ONLY NATURAL HE'D GO ALL THE WAY AND ***GROW HIMSELF A SET OF BOOBS***, TOO, HUH?!
WELL, *UM*, I... I GUESS SO...? MAYBE HE'D... I MEAN, THEY ***SAID***...er... PRETTY AMAZING, HUH?!
??

YOU USELESS LITTLE JERK!
JESUS CHRIST...
CAN'T I EVEN TRUST YOU TO GIVE ME DECENT INFORMATION?!
IT'S NOT MY FAULT! I SWEAR!! OUR CONTACT SAID "DRESSED AS A WOMAN FOR SURE"...!

HUH?! YOU STILL MAKING EXCUSES...?
TAK TAK
NO... NO... IT IS ABSOLUTELY MY FAULT... IN EVERY WAY...

WE HEARD THE ITTŌ-RYŪ DOESN'T HAVE ANY FEMALE STAFF.
AND YOU.

I... I'M A SHINZŌ*, MA'AM.
WITH THE P-PLEASURE HOUSE ITTŌ-RYŪ LIKES TO USE...

*: A YOUNG PROSTITUTE

HUH? A BROTHEL?!
YES, MA'AM... IT'S CALLED YUKI-MACHI.
WE LOAN OUR SPARE ROOMS TO THE KENSHI THEY CALL IN FROM OUT OF TOWN.

THEY GET ROOM AND BOARD, AND IN EXCHANGE...
...IF WE NEED A BOUNCER OR SOMETHING, THEY TAKE CARE OF IT.

GAAH!

AHH OGH!!

HE'D SEND SOME POOR YOUNG HOOKER INTO A MESS LIKE THIS... *DAMN!*
ANOTSU KAGEHISA, YOU'RE REALLY STARTING TO *PISS ME OFF!*

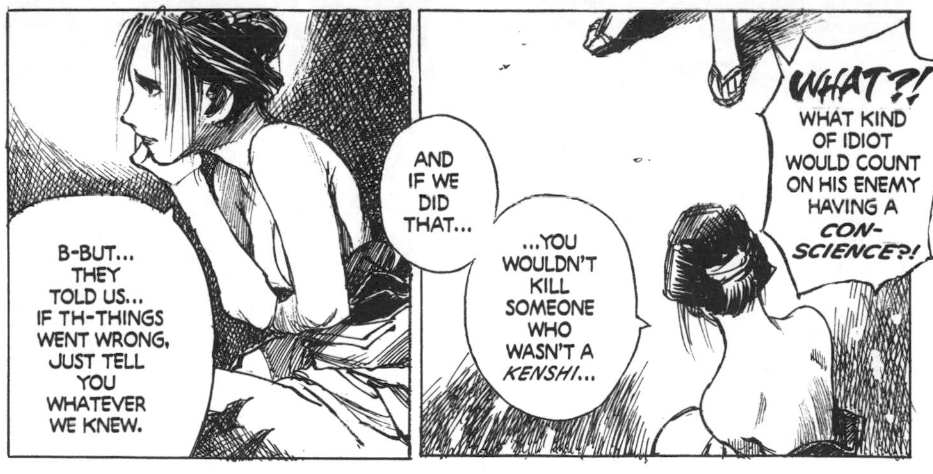
B-BUT... THEY TOLD US... IF TH-THINGS WENT WRONG, JUST TELL YOU WHATEVER WE KNEW.
AND IF WE DID THAT...
...YOU WOULDN'T KILL SOMEONE WHO WASN'T A *KENSHI*...
WHAT?! WHAT KIND OF IDIOT WOULD COUNT ON HIS ENEMY HAVING A *CON-SCIENCE?!*

LEMME TELL YOU SOMETHING, SWEETHEART.
IN THIS WORLD...
...THERE ARE SOME PSYCHOTIC BASTARDS YOUR LITTLE BOY LEADER CAN'T EVEN *BEGIN* TO IMAGINE!

AAA!
AAHN!
OUUU AAAHG!

WHUD

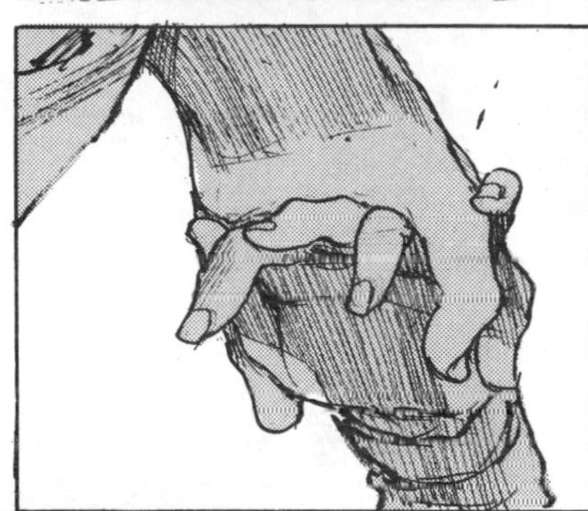

NO WAY.

I... AAH!
N- NO... *PLEASE*... FORGIVE ME...

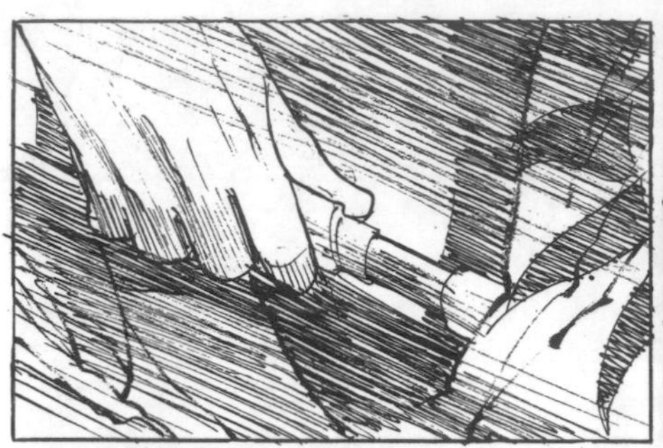

CHOK

AAH!

NO, SHIRA! STOP!

NYEH, HEH, HEH...

WHAT THE...? YOU AGAIN...?
LOOK, SHIRA-- YOU MUST BE SATISFIED NOW, RIGHT?! LET'S JUST GO! OKAY...?

SO WE FAILED-- IT WAS JUST BAD LUCK. IT WASN'T OUR FAULT!
WE'LL WAIT AND TRY AGAIN... RIGHT?!

SHE'S ONLY HERE BECAUSE ANOTSU HIRED HER, THAT'S ALL. YOU DON'T...
I MEAN... WHY DO YOU HAVE TO KILL THIS WOMAN?

RIGHT...?

KRAK

FUCK THAT SHIT!

THAT'S *TWICE* I'VE TOLD YOU.

ONE THING YOU BETTER KNOW ABOUT ME.

THERE'S NOTHING... ***NOTHING*** I HATE MORE THAN LECTURES FROM SOME DAMN ***BRAT!***

NOW KEEP YOUR GOD DAMN MOUTH ***SHUT!***

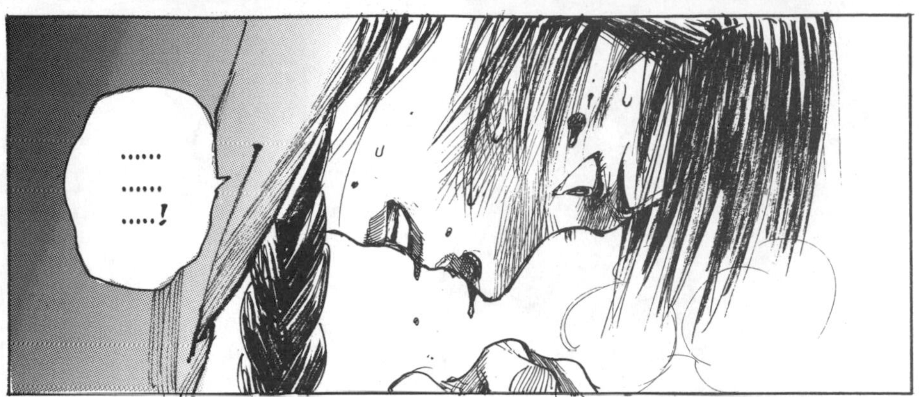

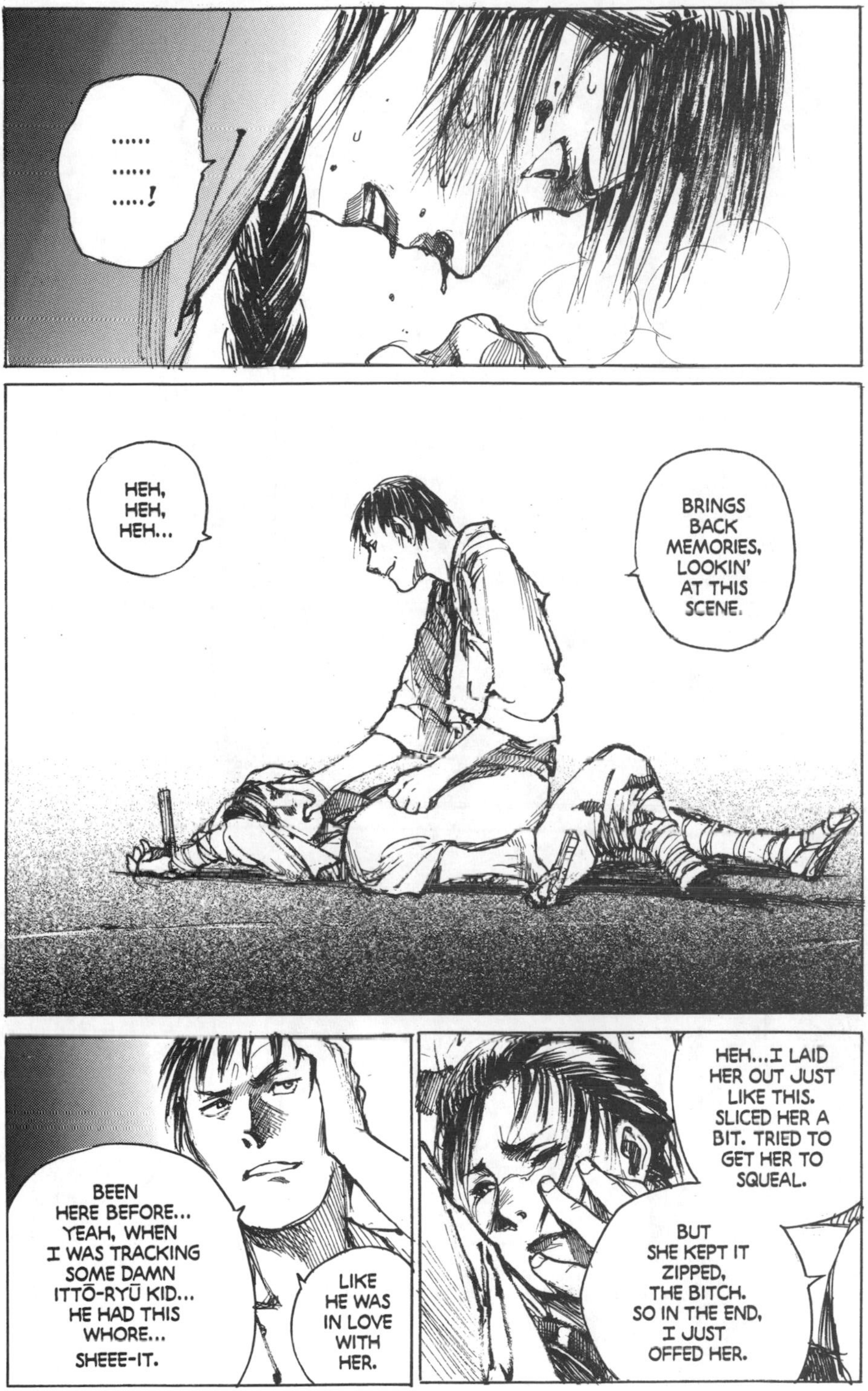

......
......
......!

HEH, HEH, HEH...
BRINGS BACK MEMORIES, LOOKIN' AT THIS SCENE.

BEEN HERE BEFORE... YEAH, WHEN I WAS TRACKING SOME DAMN ITTŌ-RYŪ KID... HE HAD THIS WHORE... SHEEE-IT.
LIKE HE WAS IN LOVE WITH HER.

HEH...I LAID HER OUT JUST LIKE THIS. SLICED HER A BIT. TRIED TO GET HER TO SQUEAL.
BUT SHE KEPT IT ZIPPED, THE BITCH. SO IN THE END, I JUST OFFED HER.

I'M NOT A *TOTAL* MONSTER, HEY? THOUGH WHEN I DID HER, IT KINDA OCCURRED TO ME, YOU KNOW?
"SHIRA, MY MAN-- YOU'RE ONE *CRUEL-ASS* DUDE! *BWA HAW HAW!*"
OR SOMETHING LIKE THAT.
BUT TODAY... TODAY I DON'T FEEL *NOTHIN'*. SO, YOU WANT TO HATE SOMEONE, SLUT...

...*HATE YOUR FRIGGIN' BOSS!*
GUESS HE DIDN'T THINK ABOUT WHAT MIGHT HAPPEN TO YOU, HEY?

HEY...?
GLOOK
AAHH!
WHOA! STINGS A BIT, EH? SORRY 'BOUT THAT. *BWA HAW HAW!*

!!
LET'S SEE WHAT YOU GOT.
C'MON--YOU'RE A ***WHORE***, RIGHT?! DON'T YA KNOW "THE CUSTOMER IS ALWAYS RIGHT"...?
EH?
N-NO... D-DON'T!
AAH!

AA...!
OH, GOD...
P- PLEASE... NO... PLEASE DON'T...

HFF

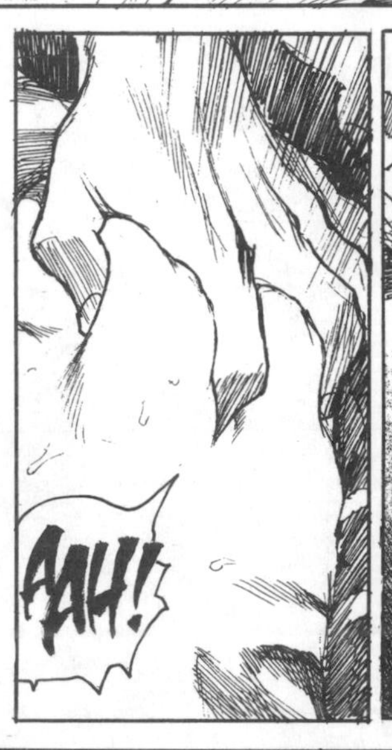
AAH!

......?!

SLOCH

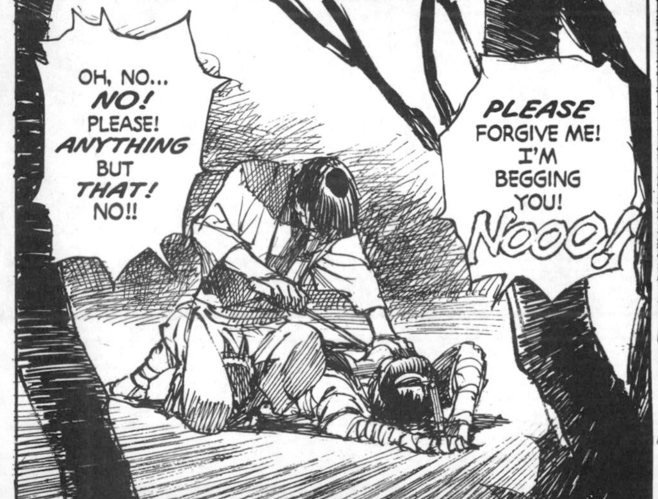
PLEASE FORGIVE ME! I'M BEGGING YOU!
NOOO!
OH, NO... NO! PLEASE! ANYTHING BUT THAT! NO!!

NNNN AAAAGH!!

NYA HAHA! PERFECT! YOU GOT IT!
WHEN A WOMAN'S WRITHING IN PAIN, HER STOMACH JERKING LIKE THAT...

...IT'S EXQUISITE!! LIKE WATCHING A SNAKE DIE...

I'LL MAKE YOU FEEL ***REAL*** GOOD, BABE... I ***WILL***.

I'D HATE IT IF YOU GOT ALL THE PAIN AND NO PLEASURE.

N-
NO...
NO...

hahh
hahh
hff
huhh

YOU KNOW...
FROM THE DAY I MET YOU...
hahh
hiff
huhh
...SHIRA...

I'VE FOLLOWED WHAT YOU DO WITH THESE EYES... WATCHED EVERYTHING.
STUDIED WHAT IT IS THAT *YOU* HAVE... AND MANJI DOESN'T.

I CAN'T FIND THE WORDS, BUT...
WHEN YOU FED ME THE DOG I'D BEFRIENDED... AND WHEN I WATCHED HOW YOU FOUGHT JUST NOW...

I FELT LIKE THROWING UP. BUT... BUT *SOME-HOW*...
...I FELT LIKE YOU WERE TEACHING ME SOMETHING I LACKED, TOO.

BUT NOW, SEEING THIS... AT LAST I KNOW.

I WAS ***WRONG.*** ***COM-PLETELY*** WRONG!

I...

I'VE BEEN TRYING HARD. TRYING TO THINK OF YOU, SHIRA...

...AS MY COMRADE-IN-ARMS.

BUT THE TRUTH IS...

I DESPISE PEOPLE LIKE YOU!!
STRIPPING AND TORTURING AN UNARMED WOMAN! HAH! YOU ENJOY THAT?!
YOU'RE JUST THE SAME!
THE SAME AS THE ITTŌ-RYŪ BASTARDS I HATE!!

......
......
YOU ALL DONE NOW?

THEN *SHUDDUP* AND *SIDDOWN.*
HOW CAN I HAVE ANY FUN WITH YOU WHINING AND SNIVELING AROUND BEHIND ME?

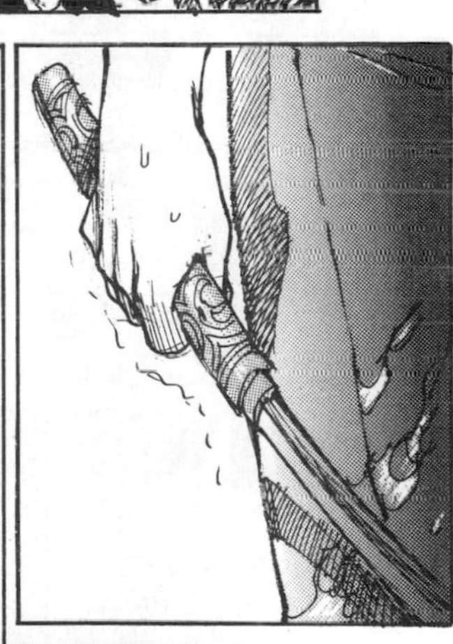

OKAY... OKAY.
THAT'S *IT.*

hnnf!

GCHOK

WHA... WHAT THE FUCK ?!

H- HOLY SHIT!

MANJI...
?!
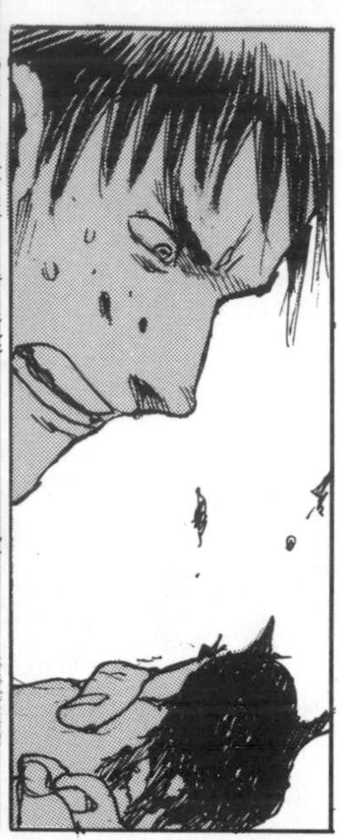
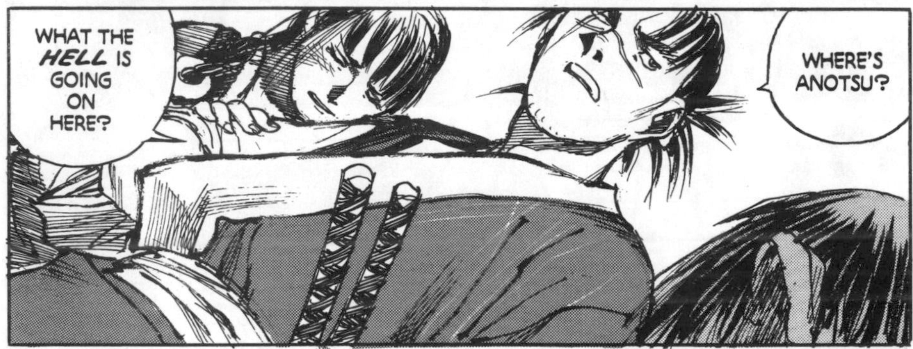
WHERE'S ANOTSU?
WHAT THE HELL IS GOING ON HERE?

STRIPPING SOME POOR WOMAN...?
JESUS, SHIRA... WHAT IS THIS SHIT?

......
......!

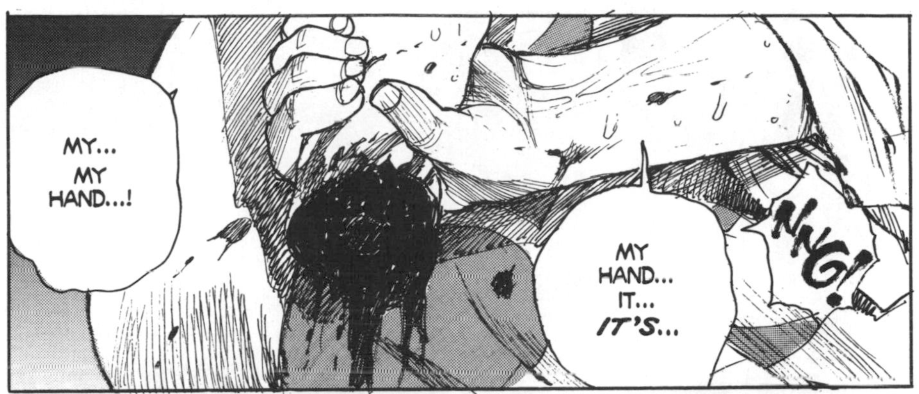
NNG!
MY HAND... IT... IT'S...
MY... MY HAND...!

UWAAA!
GOOD GOD!
TH- THERE!
M- MAYBE NOW YOU'LL--

MUH...
MANJI!!!
.....
.....

M-M- MURDERERS!!
EEEEK!

!

hahh
hff
huhh

HUH?

IF THAT CRAZY BASTARD GETS AWAY...
HEY! WAIT A SEC!!

OKAY, RIN-- WE'RE OUTTA HERE.
...ANYONE WHO SEES THIS'LL THINK I DID IT!
HUH...? BUT... WAIT...

SHRIKK

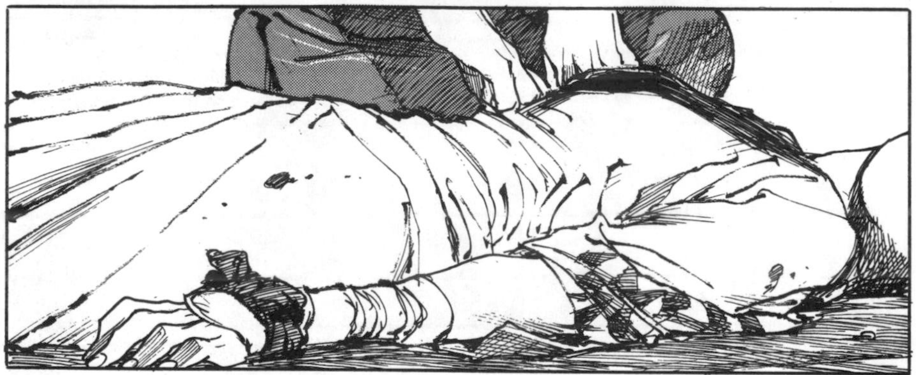

DO... DO YOU THINK SHE'LL MAKE IT?

HANDS OF FATE, RIN.

DAMN... WE CAN'T USE THE ROAD NOW.
NO CHOICE. IT'S THE FOREST, AWAY FROM SHIRA.
...... RIGHT.

DAMN IT.
DAMN IT ALL...

IBANE SHINAN-JO... DŌJŌ OF THE SHINGYŌTŌ-RYŪ SCHOOL.

CORRECT...?

YES, SIR.

HNNE!
WHDD

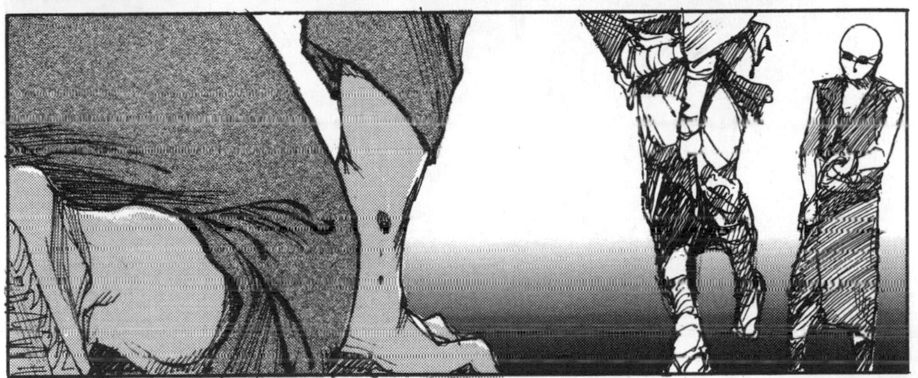

OH, DARLING... NOT *THAT!*
HE *TOLD* US NOT TO TELL THEM WHERE HE'S GOING!
FORGIVE ME, HAYA...

...BUT I COULDN'T JUST WATCH YOU DIE.
AND IF I TRIED TO SAVE YOU BY MY SWORD...

THIS MAN... HE...
KSHIK
HE'S TOO FAR BEYOND ME.

I... I'M SORRY. MY WEAKNESS...
...MADE ME SELL OUT MY COMRADES.
DAMN IT!!

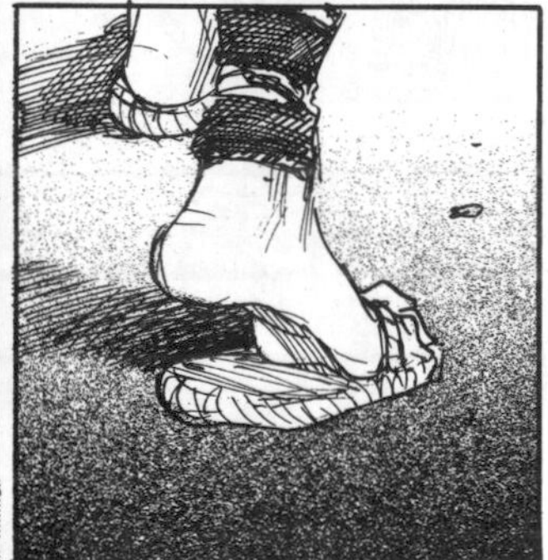

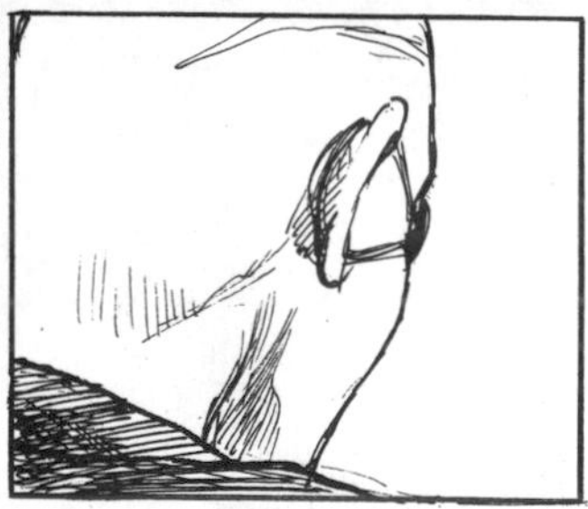

IF YOU WERE STRONGER...
...I DON'T KNOW HOW THIS WOULD HAVE ENDED. BUT I KNOW ONE THING.

THAT WOMAN WOULD BE *DEAD*.

THOSE WHO GAIN POWER...
...MUST PAY A PRICE, SOMETHING IN EXCHANGE.

IF YOU SEEK TO BE STRONGER THAN OTHERS...
...YOU MAY HAVE TO LOSE WHAT YOU VALUE ABOVE ALL ELSE.

REMEMBER THIS WELL.

GLOSSARY

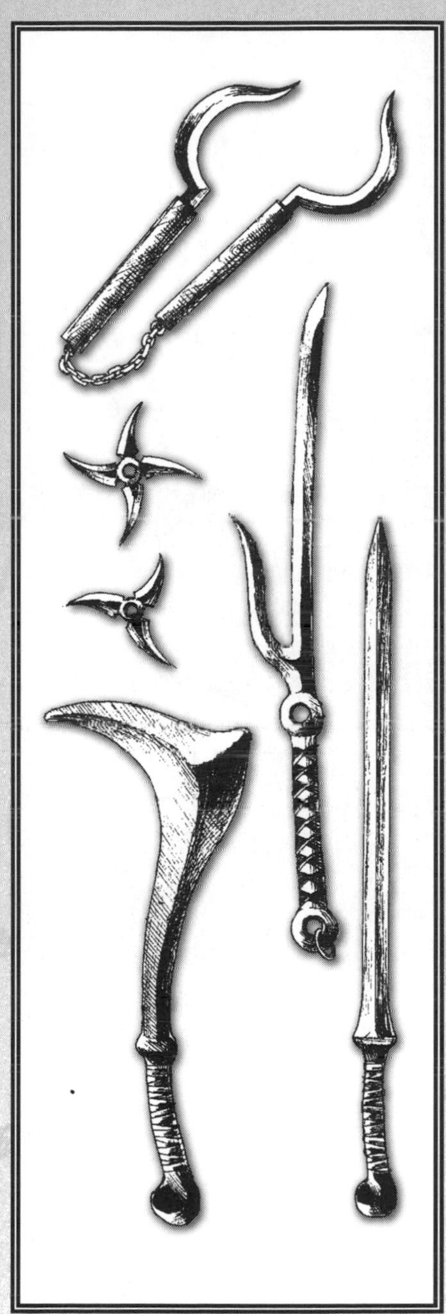

ada-uchi: to track down and kill one's enemy. An act of private vengeance, similar to nineteenth-century duels of honor. Such revenge was legal if approved by the *bugyōjō* and registered with the *hantei-jo*.

bakufu: the central government, the bureaucracy that grew up around the Tokugawa Shogunate. Originally established in Edo by the warlord Tokugawa Ieyasu.

banshi: duty officers; in this case, samurai on duty at the *sekisho*

bugyōjō: the Edo-era equivalent of a police precinct station. The *bugyō* was a high-ranked samurai in charge of keeping the peace, with the help of the men under his command and volunteer "posse" members.

daimyō: lords of provincial feudal fiefs known as *han*

de-onna: "departing woman," a woman leaving Edo. Households of important *daimyō* in distant fiefs were often required to relocate to Edo, essentially as hostages to prevent the *daimyō* from rebelling. A woman of the samurai caste travelling out of Edo could be the wife of a *daimyō* escaping, and therefore such women were checked even more strictly than the usual travelers.

dōjō: a hall for martial arts training

Edo: capital of pre-modern Japan, later renamed Tokyo

hantei-jo: an official ruling of the court

Ittō-ryū: radical sword school of Anotsu Kagehisa

kenshi: swordsman (or swordswoman)

kō: companions getting together to visit temples or take in the sights

meshimori-onna: basically, a serving wench, but one expected to perform sexual favors on the side

Mugai-ryū: sword school of the Akagi assassins; literally, "without form"

Mutenichi-ryū: sword school led by Rin's father

Naito Shinjuku: at the time, a way station on the main road west out of Edo. Today a few temple buildings and other remnants remain in Shinjuku Ni-chōme, deep within the limits of modern Tokyo.

obi: a richly embroidered sash used to close a kimono

Okabasho: all red-light districts in Edo other than Yoshiwara

ri: old Japanese unit of measurement equivalent to 2.44 miles

rōnin: a masterless samurai

ryō: a gold piece

sekisho: checkpoint. The central government strictly regulated travel, and all travelers had to submit papers at official checkpoints along the main highways into and out of Edo.

shihan: an instructor of the sword

shinan-jo: training center; *dōjō*

Shingyōtō-ryū: a variety of swordsmanship

shinzō: a young prostitute

Shi-shuku: four areas of old Edo known for their lodgings for travelers but better known as unofficial red-light districts. The four districts (still in existence today in Tokyo, although much transformed) were Shinagawa, Shinjuku, Itabashi, and Senju.

yamabaki: a woman's straw traveling hat for keeping off the sun

Yamato Takeru: a legendary hero, much beloved of Kabuki audiences. Usually portrayed in garish costumes.

yōkan: a sweet jellied bean cake. Better than it sounds.

BLADE
OF THE IMMORTAL
VISCERAL STORYTELLING
FROM MANGA MASTER
HIROAKI
SAMURA!
Volume 1: Blood of a Thousand
ISBN: 1-56971-239-5 / $14.95
Volume 2: Cry of the Worm
ISBN: 1-56971-300-6 / $14.95
Volume 3: Dreamsong
ISBN: 1-56971-357-X / $14.95
Volume 4: On Silent Wings
1-56971-412-6 / $14.95
Volume 5: On Silent Wings II
1-56971-444-4 / $14.95
Volume 6:Dark Shadows
1-56971 469 X / $14.95
Volume 7: Heart of Darkness
1-56971-531-9 / $16.95
Volume 8: The Gathering
1-56971-546-7 / $15.95
Volume 9: The Gathering II
1-56971-560-2 / $15.95
Volume 10: Secrets
1-56971-746-X / $16.95
Volume 11: Beasts
1-56971-741-9 / $14.95
Volume 12: Autumn Frost
1-56971-991-8 / $16.95
Volume 13: Mirror of the Soul
1-59307-218-X / $17.95
Volume 14: Last Blood
1-59307-321-6 / $17.95
Available at your local
comics shop or bookstore!
To find a comics shop in your area,
call 1-888-266-4226
For more information or to order direct
visit Darkhorse.com or call
1-800-862-0052 Mon.-Sat.
9 A.M. to 5 P.M. Pacific Time
*Prices and availability subject to change without notice
Blade of the Immortal copyright © 2005 by Hiroaki Samura. All rights reserved. Dark Horse Manga™ is a trademark of Dark Horse Comics, Inc. All rights reserved.
EISNER AWARD WINNER
DARK HORSE MANGA

DON'T MISS THESE OTHER FANTASTIC TITLES FROM DARK HORSE MANGA AND STUDIO PROTEUS!

AKIRA
Katsuhiro Otomo

Book 1
364-page B&W / 1-56971-498-3 / $24.95

Book 2
304-page B&W / 1-56971-499-1 / $24.95

Book 3
288-page B&W / 1-56971-525-4 / $24.95

Book 4
400-page B&W / 1-56971-526-2 / $27.95

Book 5
416-page B&W / 1-56971-527-0 / $27.95

Book 6
440-page B&W / 1-56971-528-9 / $29.95

ASTRO BOY
Osamu Tezuka

Volume 1
224-page B&W / 1-56971-676-5 / $9.95

Volume 2
208-page B&W / 1-56971-677-3 / $9.95

Volume 3
208-page B&W / 1-56971-678-1 / $9.95

Volume 4
216-page B&W / 1-56971-679-X / $9.95

Volume 5
216-page B&W / 1-56971-680-3 / $9.95

Volume 6
232-page B&W / 1-56971-681-1 / $9.95

Volume 7
216-page B&W / 1-56971-790-7 / $9.95

Volume 8
200-page B&W / 1-56971-791-5 / $9.95

Volume 9
216-page B&W / 1-56971-792-3 / $9.95

Volume 10
216-page B&W / 1-56971-793-1 / $9.95

Volume 11
216-page B&W / 1-56971-812-1 / $9.95

Volume 12
224-page B&W / 1-56971-813-X / $9.95

Volume 13
224-page B&W / 1-56971-894-6 / $9.95

Volume 14
224-page B&W / 1-56971-895-4 / $9.95

Volume 15
232-page B&W / 1-56971-896-2 / $9.95

Volume 16
256-page B&W / 1-56971-897-0 / $9.95

Volume 17
216-page B&W / 1-56971-898-9/ $9.95

Volume 18
216-page B&W / 1-56971-899-7 /$9.95

Volume 19
216-page B&W / 1-56971-900-4 / $9.95

Volume 20
224-page B&W / 1-56971-901-2 / $9.95

Volume 21
232-page B&W / 1-56971-902-0 / $9.95

Volume 22
216-page B&W / 1-56971-903-9 / $9.95

Volume 23
192-page B&W / 1-59307-135-3 /$9.95

BLADE OF THE IMMORTAL
Hiroaki Samura

Volume 1: Blood of a Thousand
192-page B&W / 1-56971-239-5 / $14.95

Volume 2: Cry of the Worm
176-page B&W / 1-56971-300-6 / $14.95

Volume 3: Dreamsong
208-page B&W / 1-56971-357-X / $14.95

Volume 4: On Silent Wings
176-page B&W / 1-56971-412-6 / $14.95

Volume 5: On Silent Wings II
184-page B&W / -56971-444-4 / $14.95

Volume 6: Dark Shadows
192-page B&W / 1-56971-469-X / $14.95

Volume 7: Heart of Darkness
192-page B&W / 1-56971-531-9 / $16.95

Volume 8: The Gathering
208-page B&W / 1-56971-546-7 / $15.95

Volume 9: The Gathering II
216-page B&W / 1-56971-560-2 / $15.95

Volume 10: Secrets
232-page B&W / 1-56971-746-X / $16.95

Volume 11: Beasts
192-page B&W / 1-56971-741-9 / $14.95

Volume 12: Autumn Frost
232-page B&W / 1-56971-991-8 / $16.95

Volume 13: Mirror of the Soul
256-page B&W / 1-59307-218-X / $17.95

GUNSMITH CATS
Kenichi Sonoda

Volume 1: Bonnie and Clyde
176-page B&W / 1-56971-215-8 / $13.95

Volume 2: Misfire
184-page B&W / 1-56971-253-0 / $14.95

Volume 3: The Return of Gray
248-page B&W / 1-56971-299-9 / $17.95

Volume 4: Goldie vs. Misty
192-page B&W / 1-56971-371-5 / $15.95

Volume 5: Bad Trip
170-page B&W / 1-56971-442-8 / $13.95

Volume 6: Bean Bandit
224-page B&W / 1-56971-453-3 / $16.95

Volume 7: Kidnapped
232-page B&W / 1-56971-529-7 / $16.95

Volume 8: Mr. V
224-page B&W / 1-56971-550-5 / $18.95

Volume 9: Misty's Run
176-page B&W / 1-56971-684-6 / $14.95

LONE WOLF AND CUB
Kazuo Koike and Goseki Kojima

Volume 1: The Assassin's Road
296-page B&W / 1-56971-502-5 / $9.95

Volume 2: The Gateless Barrier
296-page B&W / 1-56971-503-3 / $9.95

Volume 3: The Flute of the Fallen Tiger
304-page B&W / 1-56971-504-1 / $9.95

Volume 4: The Bell Warden
304-page B&W / 1-56971-505-X / $9.95

Volume 5: Black Wind
288-page B&W / 1-56971-506-8 / $9.95

Volume 6: Lanterns for the Dead
288-page B&W / 1-56971-507-6 / $9.95

Volume 7: Cloud Dragon, Wind Tiger
320-page B&W / 1-56971-508-4 / $9.95

Volume 8: Chains of Death
304-page B&W / 1-56971-509-2 / $9.95

Volume 9: Echo of the Assassin
288-page B&W / 1-56971-510-6 / $9.95

Volume 10: Hostage Child
320-page B&W / 1-56971-511-4 / $9.95

Volume 11: Talisman of Hades
320-page B&W / 1-56971-512-2 / $9.95

Volume 12: Shattered Stones
304-page B&W / 1-56971-513-0 / $9.95

Volume 13: The Moon in the East, The Sun in the West
320-page B&W / 1-56971-585-8 / $9.95

Volume 14: The Day of the Demons
320-page B&W / 1-56971-586-6 / $9.95

Volume 15: Brothers of the Grass
352-page B&W / 1-56971-587-4 / $9.95

Volume 16: Gateway into Winter
320-page B&W / 1-56971-588-2 / $9.95

Volume 17: The Will of the Fang
320-page B&W / 1-56971-589-0 / $9.95

Volume 18: Twilight of the Kurokuwa
320-page B&W / 1-56971-590-4 / $9.95

Volume 19: The Moon in Our Hearts
320-page B&W / 1-56971-591-2 / $9.95

Volume 20: A Taste of Poison
320-page B&W / 1-56971-592-0 / $9.95

Volume 21: Fragrance of Death
320-page B&W / 1-56971-593-9 / $9.95

Volume 22: Heaven and Earth
288-page B&W / 1-56971-594-7 / $9.95

Volume 23: Tears of Ice
320-page B&W / 1-56971-595-5 / $9.95

Volume 24: In These Small Hands
320-page B&W / 1-56971-596-3 / $9.95

Volume 25: Perhaps in Death
320-page B&W / 1-56971-597-1 / $9.95

Volume 26: Struggle in the Dark
312-page B&W / 1-56971-598-X / $9.95

Volume 27: Battle's Eve
300-page B&W / 1-56971-599-8 / $9.95

Volume 28: The Lotus Throne
320-page B&W / 1-56971-600-5 / $9.95

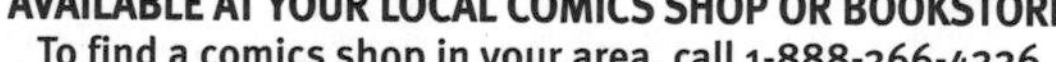

AVAILABLE AT YOUR LOCAL COMICS SHOP OR BOOKSTORE

To find a comics shop in your area, call 1-888-266-4226

For more information or to order direct: • On the web: www.darkhorse.com • E-mail: mailorder@darkhorse.com
• Phone: 1-800-862-0052 or (503) 652-9701 Mon.-Sat. 9 A.M. to 5 P.M. Pacific Time